AWAKENING THE BOLD

THE PROPHETIC LEADERSHIP MANDATE

"The fog is dissipating
I prophesy clarity in vision + discernment"

Ulrich Tofack

ULRICH TOFACK

Copyright © 2022 Ulrich Tofack

ROYAL HEIRS MINISTRIES

All rights reserved. No part of this book may be reproduced or transmitted in any form or by any means, electronic or mechanical, including photocopying, recording, or by any information storage and retrieval system without express written permission from the author / publisher.

Unless otherwise identified, Scripture quotations are taken from the Complete Jewish Study Bible, Copyright © 2016, by Hendrickson Publishers. Used with permission. Scripture quotations marked NET are taken from the NET Online Bible (www.netbible.org). Used with permission. Scripture quotations marked KJV are taken from Blue Letter Bible (www.blueletterbible.org). Used with permission. Scripture quotations marked NIV are taken from The NIV Study Bible Copyright © 1985, by Zondervan. Used with permission. Scripture quotations marked AMP are taken from The Amplified Holy Bible Copyright © 2016, by The Lockman Foundation. Used with permission.

CONTENTS

Preface v
Dedication vii
Acknowledgements...................................... ix
Endorsements.. xiii
Foreword.. xv
Introduction xvii

PART ONE: THE FOUNDATION 1
Chapter 1. What Is Prophetic Leadership?................. 3
Chapter 2. Opposite Forces............................. 14
Chapter 3. History Rhymes 22
Chapter 4. The Lord's Two-Fold Vision 30

**PART TWO: THE MAKING OF
A PROPHETIC LEADER**............................ 43
Chapter 1. Separating Identity From Familiarity 45
Chapter 2. Brokenness 57
Chapter 3. Walking In Repentance....................... 77
Chapter 4. Wilderness And Trials........................ 86
Chapter 5. Intimacy: The Source Of Prophetic Leadership 99

PART THREE: CULTIVATING PROPHETIC LEADERSHIP **113**

Chapter 1. Prophetic Purpose 115
Chapter 2. Cultivating Prophetic Vision 134
Chapter 3. Practical Guidelines 155
Chapter 4. Marching Orders 166

Conclusion 175
Afterword 179
Bibliography 183
Endnotes 187

PREFACE

Prophetic people must awaken to a resolute sense of divine destiny, which is the catalyst for us to fulfill the Lord's purposes in our generation. Looking back at biblical and world history, it is easy to be overwhelmed by the exploits that many ordinary men accomplished under God's extraordinary leadership. Yet there seems to be a lack of courage among the church ranks today.

For the church to champion the cultural revolution that the Lord intends in our generation, there is a desperate need for a company of prophetic people to emerge on the face of the earth that are radically consecrated unto the Lord and devoted to overthrow the status quo in their sphere of influence. The time is now, as the clash between the kingdoms of Light and darkness is coming to a climax.

DEDICATION

First, to my heavenly Father, to Whom I owe everything. To Jesus Christ, Who took me out of perdition and loves me so much more than I could ever fathom. To Holy Spirit, Who shows great patience towards me daily, and Who found me worthy to be entrusted with such revelation. I love You Holy Spirit, and I hope I was able to convey the heart of the Father faithfully.

To my wife, Rebecca, you have stood with me through thick and thin. I know the depth of the sacrifices you have made for the sake of the Kingdom. Great is your reward here on earth and in the age to come. You are the best helpmate and encourager I could ever have; I love you. To our children, you bring me such joy and I know the plans that the Lord has for you: even greater works shall you do indeed.

To those who feel discouraged, who feel like they have lost their way, who are misunderstood, looked down upon, discounted, uncertain about their lives' significance, let this book be an invitation to the unshakable hope that you have in Christ Jesus.

ACKNOWLEDGEMENTS

Authoring this book was not the easiest thing for me to do, as I often wrote during times of intense pressure, pain, and opposition. Therefore, I want to acknowledge those who have been instrumental in my life journey up to this point.

My spiritual father Prophet William Undi, I am forever thankful to you and your ministry. I thank God that you obeyed the Lord in the summer of 2019, calling me out from delaying the call of God upon my life, and exhorting me to fully embrace it. Your obedience saved my life, literally. Your life is a testament of true love and humility. Thank you for encouraging me to persevere in trying times, for speaking into my life as a prophetic father, and for confirming me into the five-fold office of a prophet to the nations by the laying of the hands on me, my wife, and our children in the presence of The Beloved Church family.

My other spiritual father, Tim Dziomba. You have spoken to my manhood in ways I cannot describe. Your counsel has made me a better man, husband, and father, you are a gift to me and to men. A few minutes after receiving the Word of the Lord by Prophet William on that fateful summer in 2019, you walked up to me by divine appointment, ditched your busy schedule and sat with me for the next 3 hours, praying and comforting me with tears. I am blessed and honored to call you both my fathers in the faith.

The late Pastor R. Loren Sandford who personally mentored me during his last days on earth. The late Prophet David Wilkerson for establishing me in sound doctrine during my early walk with the Lord. The late Dr. Myles Munroe and Prophet Kobus Van Rensburg for the deep spiritual heritage I am benefiting from. Rick Joyner and Michael Fickess, for your personal mentoring in writing and leadership. Dr. Jorge Parrott, and Dr. Nancy Daniel at CMM World Missions, for believing in me. Pastors Max and Célestiane Vogné, for your genuine labor of love and support in my life. Apostle Joshua Giles: you inspire me.

My brothers in the Lord: Steve Ekholm, Eliakim Ballé, Devin Amberg, Holali Amevor, Jonathan Ouedraogo, Eric Sponheim, Kevin Gustafson, Marcus Butler, Jason Wood, Josh Bohlen. I am grateful for your lives.

My spiritual daughter, Stella Grosjean in Switzerland, for being the first fruit of my labor in the Lord. What a blessing to see your spiritual and character transformation over the past 7 years: glorious is the destiny ahead of you. My sisters in the Lord, Jeannette Hillaire and Grace Ouedraogo: you should have shown up in our lives sooner. Prophetess Dee Giles: I bless the Lord for your life. To Julie Berntson, a true mother in the Lord: I love you.

To my earthly father and mother, to my father and mother-in-law, thank you for your care, patience, and love. To my brothers and sisters-in-law, I bless you.

ACKNOWLEDGEMENTS

To our ministry's financial partners and anyone that has sowed into our lives and ministry, I thank you for your prayers and for your continued financial support: your harvest will be great.

May you and those I have omitted, all be richly blessed, in Christ Jesus.

ENDORSEMENTS

There is no greater testimony of the formidable truths printed in this book than the evidence in the author's own life! I've had the privilege of becoming a mentor of Prophet Ulrich and have observed him live out the truths he shares in this book, resulting in success, leading to Jesus being glorified.

This book is sound, easy to read and authoritative – flooded with truths that equip and impart one to be a prophetic leader. I believe this book can be used as a handbook to train and lead prophets. I definitely recommend it to everyone who desires to prophesy and lead prophetic lives. May Jesus be glorified as you are awakened by Spirit filled writings in this book.

Man sent from God!
William Caleb Undi
The Beloved Church, Johannesburg, South Africa
www.thebelovedtv.org

Ulrich Tofack is a close friend, minister, and prophetic encourager. He speaks prophetic potential in believers and anyone the Lord brings to him. He stokes fires of revival wherever he goes. This book, *Awakening the Bold*, will fan the flame of transformation & prophetic destiny in your life!

Steve Ekholm
Lead Pastor, Living Hope Church, MN, USA
www.livinghopechurchmora.com

FOREWORD

Dr. Ulrich Tofack and I were first acquainted while studying our Doctor of Theology at CMM College of Theology. As our time in our studies progressed it was not long before I was aware we shared a similar fire, passion and intensity for the prophetic ministry and calling. It was noticeably clear we held a kindred spirit so to speak, regarding our approach to truth and the scriptures.

As a prophetic leader myself, I can undeniably say the need for sound, solid, discipleship in the prophetic community is at an all-time high. Many books have been written on the "gifting" of the prophetic or the "prophetic anointings," but very few on the topic of prophetic leadership. Teaching and training people in the "ways" of God seem to be a missing element in recent times and more of an emphasis has been placed on the gifts and callings. The fruit of this has developed a slightly out of balance prophetic community that have cultivated gifting over character. When this is the case, we run into all sorts of trouble as the "integrity" of the prophetic comes into question. *"Awakening the Bold – The Prophetic Leadership Mandate,"* however, serves as an antidote to this imbalance, being a prophetic manual that will equip you to understand the "ways" of God in Kingdom leadership and the purpose and function of the prophetic in bringing the purposes of

God to pass in the earth. When we have teaching on these realms, we have a true equipping that produces maturity in the believer.

This writing draws the reader's attention to the urgency of the hour and how in order for the church to fulfill her destiny, the understanding and rise of prophetic leadership is key. With the anointing of a true prophetic scalpel Ulrich can help you see plainly the importance of the link to leadership and destiny. This book is provoking, convicting and is a well explained map of A-Z in the prophetic and leadership. The weight and the substance in the writing keeps the reader wanting more as each chapter evolves.

Ulrich's straight-shooting, no-nonsense delivery has the sense of a military trumpet that is booming out of the throne room in this crucial hour, calling the Lord's people to position themselves. Truly, the unlocking of what it is to "follow" the Lord is essential to know, then how to "lead" before the Lord. I enjoyed how Ulrich puts it in the conclusion of this writing, *"He (the Lord) trains men to walk before Him before He can release them to walk before men. This means that ultimately prophetic leaders are not only concerned about the fulfilment of their individual assignment on the earth. They understand that the heavens rejoice the more when their lives become a gift to humanity."*

I encourage you to take time in the study of these pages as you digest the truths delivered. Without a doubt you will discover that your understanding of the ways of God have matured and expanded empowering you forward into destiny.

Dr. Anita Alexander
Prophetic Revivalist, Author, Co- Senior Minister Golden City Church,
Gold Coast, Qld
Australia.

INTRODUCTION

The hour for the greatest leaders of the church's modern era to emerge has finally arrived. It may sound cliche, but seriously. Before disqualifying yourself by closing this book and returning to a life of insignificance, it is important for you to realize that if you are walking in the Kingdom of God, your earthly reality is not always a reflection of Truth.

An honest assessment of the present reality around us is precisely what will make the following truth self-evident: you were purposefully created for such a time, and then dropped behind enemy's lines as a foolproof weapon fashioned by the hand of God.

The world is starving for the kind of people who can boldly speak and live with prophetic vision. Looking back at biblical and world history, it is easy to be overwhelmed by the multitude of exploits accomplished by ordinary men under God's extraordinary leadership. Yet, there seems to be a strange lack of courage in the church ranks today.

Unfortunately, this cowardice is characterized by the apathy that still exists in the church despite numerous wake up calls within the past couple of years. The idea that impactful leadership within the church's ranks is reserved for those who hold a microphone behind a pulpit has made us less effective in facing modern challenges.

For the church to have the impact that the Lord intends in our generation, there is a desperate need for people to emerge as the agents of transformation that the world so desperately needs.

There is a divine mandate on the church – the people- to have a transformative impact in a lost and perverse generation. This mandate cannot be carried by those behind the pulpits alone, though it may start there in some cases.

It was never the Lord's intention for Church influence to be boxed in within the four walls of a house or a religious organization. Jesus Himself taught the crowds as He went and performed most of His miracles out in the marketplace. He often taught in the temple, while mostly demonstrating the power of the Kingdom of God outside of its four walls amongst the "unchurched."

By so doing, He demonstrated that producing impactful individuals who, through true discipleship, yield a powerful marching force on the face of earth is far more essential than erecting fancy buildings. Today's "church" buildings must now turn into spiritual training launching pads, instead of merely existing as glorified and compromised clubhouses.

Both biblical and world history are rich in examples of men and women that accomplished great things with faith and courage, ultimately changing the course of civilization, without ever holding the official titles and degrees that religious people think are necessary. Many of them did it without ever standing behind a pulpit. They just responded to a burden that the Lord had placed upon their hearts with resolute faith.

True prophetic people carry a heavy sense of divine destiny, and they can clearly identify the antagonistic (opposing) forces that govern the affairs of men in their spheres of influence. They are aware of the necessity to walk in their God's given purpose. They live in a way that clearly communicates the reality that it is no longer they who live, but Christ in them. Furthermore, they are not driven by personal ambition but are compelled by divine destiny.

Therefore, they walk with the conviction that their lives were created as a divine solution to a specific problem. Such people can develop penetrating vision to see into the future. They also develop the inner strength to step into unchartered territory to meet that future, with the Holy Spirit as their primary guide.

Prophetic leadership is a process that originates with God. And because He is the quintessence of true leadership, we can say that the prophetic leadership process is supernatural. It is a spiritual outworking that is meant to bring forth the Lord's purposes on the earth.

Because it is consistent with the character of God: it opposes some form of evil, serves humanity, and exalts justice and righteousness. Furthermore, it is a formidable adventure predicated on an intimate walk with the Lord. Lastly, it aims to lead or restore others to their own place of divine inheritance.

However, a careful read of the Word of the God suggests that the Lord does not entrust a significant mission or message to someone without also forging in them the character adequate to support their intended spiritual stature. This is especially true in these last days, as there is now little to no time for lukewarmness.

Unfortunately, this is a process that most well-meaning people in the church are unwilling to embrace because it requires a lifestyle rooted in unwavering trust in Christ. Very few want to pay the price that consists of the crushing of self-ambition, rejection and misunderstanding, humbling times of invisibility, spiritual discipline, and trials in the wilderness.

The majority only want the appeal of outer glory offered by talents and giftings, while rejecting the pruning process that is meant to reveal the greater glory of "Christ in us." As a result, character flaws and spiritual immaturity suffocate the impact they were meant to have in their generation.

On the other hand, some embrace the process but remain stuck in the pews because of fear. To be fair, there is a strong wind of delusion and slumber blowing in the body of Christ in general, particularly in the Western hemisphere.

This gives way to a generation of saints who may have the right intentions yet are crippled by doctrines and preachers that glamorize on-stage five-fold ministry on one hand or impose ridiculous religious yokes on people on the other. This results in producing people who are either reduced to Sunday cheerleading, or lifeless religious activities.

Because of these dynamics in the body of Christ, specifically the prophetic movement, very few understand who they are, which makes it difficult for them to embrace the process that the call of God on their lives requires. But those who can see the joy set before them beyond the cross are the overcomers that will end up fulfilling their God given mandate to prepare the way of the Lord.

Therefore, it is important to embrace the fact that any purpose originated by God inevitably leads to a transformative process that produces true spiritual character.[1] This is crucial, because without it these appointed champions cannot walk in the full extent of the grace and authority that they need to fulfill the Lord's calling in our generation.

Taking an honest look at our current sphere(s) of influence, it is easy to see that the gates of hell have been opened and that darkness is on the rise. Indeed, according to the word of God the end of the present age is characterized by gross darkness… in the world. But for any Kingdom citizen to accept that reality as the truth that governs their life is the greatest tragedy of the twenty-first century.

Make no mistake: the clash between the kingdoms of Light and darkness is coming to a climax. The church is that Light bearer. As much as gross darkness covers the earth, *our Light has indeed already come* and it is time to arise and shine, not hide.

If you managed to read up to this point, you have inched closer to resigning as a powerless and indifferent Sunday church bench warmer. Get ready to step into the unchartered waters of destiny to meet the champion that God created you to be, for such a time as this.

PART ONE

THE FOUNDATION

What is Prophetic Leadership?

| GOD'S IDEA

God thinks of leadership from a much higher plane than man. This is not surprising, considering that for Him to eternally maintain His status as LORD of Lords, His ways and His thoughts must be higher than ours.

Therefore, as the Leader of leaders and the very essence of leadership, it is important to capture the way He expresses His leadership as well as how He intends His people to lead. Should true leadership find its roots in the Creator, then it is essential to define it from His perspective.

Jesus was the perfect expression of this kind of leadership, but He was not the first, nor was He the last to be raised by God as one. Though He is the only one to do it with perfection, there were men used by God to bring forth His agenda on the earth before and after Jesus' walk on the earth. The same is true today.

The existential threat to the Lord's purposes in a generation often creates the climate suitable for God to raise such individuals. Think of men like Noah, whom God chose to preserve humanity from utter corruption. Abraham was separated from his family by God to re-establish consecration and faith-based relationship with God in a generation dominated by world-wide paganism. Joseph was handpicked by God, trained in obscurity after suffering great injustice, and was raised just in time to preserve the world from a devastating famine. The early church's Apostles were raised to bring salvation to the gentiles, without which God's Kingdom cannot be advanced to the ends of the earth. These are just a few among many examples throughout scriptures.

Modern history can point to Martin Luther, William Seymour, Nicolaus Zinzendorf, and several others whom God has used in a comparable way. A careful study of these heroes of the faith shows that they had one thing in common. They all had a resolute sense of divine destiny and God used them at critical times to preserve the Seed through which His purposes are accomplished on the earth.

However, it is important to note that throughout history God has not restrained Himself to using only those who were deemed "religious" to advance His purposes on the earth. In fact, it was never God's intent to establish religion as we know it. But this can easily be a separate book.

The Bible shows us that God used people like King Cyrus and others who did not necessarily belong to His family (the people of Israel in the Old Covenant or believers in Christ in the New Covenant), to accomplish His purposes on the earth. It is no secret that the hearts of kings are in the Lord's hand, and He turns them as He pleases.[2]

Furthermore, no earthly authority can establish itself: God must allow it otherwise it cannot be.[3]

Consider Nelson Mandela, who spent over 27 years in prison fueled by his desire to see the abolition of the Apartheid in South Africa. Abraham Lincoln put his life on the line to end slavery in America. Martin Luther King Jr. gave his life for racial equality in America. Winston Churchill stood alone against Nazism and was rejected by his own government until they realized that he was the only man with the intestinal fortitude to oppose Hitler. The list goes on.

The point is, if God's own people – the church - remain apathetic in a generation, He will find someone who is fueled by a noble desire to sacrifice their personal comfort to confront some form of evil in their generation. Even then, in every generation the Lord continues to scan the earth, seeking a man or woman after His own heart through whom He can accomplish His purposes.

This is important because as shocking as it may sound, God's priorities are not to end evil per se, to preserve a certain civilization, or even less to redeem worldly systems. In fact, the latter is an error that has crept within the body of Christ recently, so it is important that I address it here once and for all. God is not interested in redeeming worldly, manmade systems. He is primarily concerned about establishing His Kingdom on the earth and He does so through the salvation of mankind in Christ Jesus as the building stone.

Once authentic salvation occurs, it must be followed by transformative discipleship which consists of being immersed into the reality of the Kingdom of God and its advancement. If that is effectively accomplished, then righteousness will follow in our societies, for "When the righteous flourish, the people rejoice; but when the wicked are in power, the people groan." (Proverbs 29:2, CJB).

Because this contrasted reality is felt today with greater intensity than perhaps any other time in the past, it is only right to expect God to raise a standard[4] once again in our generation to preserve His seed and advance His purposes on the earth. The Lord will do it by raising a company of people that are radically consecrated unto Him. These people are devoted to confronting the status quo of evil by championing truth in their respective sphere(s) of influence.

This time around, God the Father wants to prioritize His own people for this task because there is also a great harvest at hand. With that in mind, He desires to entrust it in the hands of those who intimately know and walk with Him, to prepare the second coming of the Lord Jesus.

For God to raise such a standard in our generation, there is a divine commissioning currently taking place throughout the earth. "The night is almost over; the day is almost here. So, let us put aside the deeds of darkness and arm ourselves with the weapons of light."[5]

| THE COMMISSIONING

The Lord Jesus spoke to me four years ago, saying: "I am now raising prophetic leaders on the earth." I spent the following days researching prophetic leadership online and found little to nothing. Things became a bit scarier when He told me to not only write on the matter, but to be one that trains them as well.

I was speechless: I had never heard of it, and I did not know where to start. As a result, I did not believe I was qualified, so I ran away for a while. This could be you, running away from the call of God on your life. The marvelous thing about the Lord is that when He initiates something, He only requires us to trust in His Spirit to accomplish it and not our own ability.[6]

Following this encounter, the first thing the Holy Spirit brought to remembrance was to always evaluate every new or unfamiliar concept through His Word. With that, the Holy Spirit took me to school, and He began to unpack His word one layer at the time.

Let us start with some fundamental definitions. Prophetic leadership is made up of two words: *prophetic* and *leadership*. The word "prophetic" finds its roots in the word *"prophet,"* while leadership comes from the verb *"to lead."*

There is a commonly known principle in studying scripture called the Law of First Mention. This principle, with few exceptions, states that the first time an important word or concept is mentioned in the Bible, it often contextually reveals its fullest and/or original meaning. This principle will be referred to a few times throughout this book, so bear that in mind.

| PROPHET ('NABI)

This might sound foreign to you but from God's perspective and contrary to modern belief, at the core, a prophet is not necessarily someone who has mastered the ability to predict the future or to read someone's mail. If we were to call one a prophet based on that alone, then we might as well ask soothsayers, mediums, and new age gurus to train us because they can be much more accurate in those disciplines than most authentic prophetic people in the church today.

Growing up in Africa where witchcraft is customary practice, I know firsthand how much power and accuracy these demonic agents have. Even now in the western world, these agents are practicing publicly more boldly and because of their accuracy, many undiscerning people are led astray.

For the record, witchcraft has always existed in the western hemisphere; it was just hiding in plain sight, which is even more dangerous. Then, one may rightly ask, what is a prophet at the core, in God's eyes?

There are countless materials on prophets and regarding the prophetic ministry available. I must emphasize that this book is not an expository work on prophets, the prophetic, or prophecy. So, the following is not a comprehensive definition. However, it captures the core of a prophet from the Lord's perspective according to scripture.

We first find the word "prophet" in Genesis 20:1-7. Abraham is sojourning in the land of Gerar. Upon arrival, he pretended his wife Sarah to be his sister for fear of getting killed. Abimelech king of Gerar, seeing that she was beautiful, sent for her and wanted to take her as wife. But God rebuked him in a dream and said: "… Now return the man's wife, for he is a *prophet*, and he will pray for you, and you will live."

A meticulous study of Abraham's journey with God would reveal that up until this time in Abraham's walk, he had never spoken a word of prophecy to anyone. Furthermore, there is no direct biblical account of Abraham vocally giving prophetic words or words of knowledge to individuals or nations beyond this moment in time either.

So, how could God call this man a prophet if he had never prophesied or predicted the future by an utterance? As you can see, it becomes a bit clearer that God's definition of a prophet goes beyond prophetic utterances.

If that statement were made in modern day Christianity, some would have perhaps entertained the idea that God made a mistake by calling Abraham a prophet. Yet we know God makes no mistakes in discerning the hearts of men, while men are prone to be swayed by the outward appearance. There must have been something else on God's heart.

The word "prophet" here is the Hebrew word *'nabi'*[7], which is from a Hebrew root meaning to *"bring forth."* In the context of prophecy, we understand that it speaks of bringing forth the word of God. How could Abraham be bringing forth the Word of God without predicting the future or giving a prophetic word to someone or to a nation?

As we will see later, He was an intimate friend of God and an intercessor. But for the interest of our current discussion the reason is quite simple: Abraham heard what God said and he began to *live it out*. His life was the unfolding of a divine mandate, he was a *living epistle* way before the New Covenant Apostles awakened to that reality.

Although foretelling is important and may serve to confirm a prophetic office, the prophet's essential tasks are twofold: *forth bringing* (or *forthtelling*) God's purposes, and intercession.

In the encounter above, God revealed those essential tasks while He rebuked Abimelech. His statement could be paraphrased as such: "Abimelech, I know you do not mean evil, but your action is an existential threat to My purposes. So, to preserve the Seed through which My purposes will be accomplished on the earth, I will have no other choice but to end your life unless you obey. Therefore, return this man his wife, because I am actively working through his life to bring forth *('nabi)* my Word and my purposes on the earth. And the sign that I will use to confirm this to you is that he will pray to Me on your behalf *(intercession)*, and I will heal you."[8]

Therefore, a prophet at the core is someone who lays hold of the living Word of God, and lays down his life to bring forth, or manifest if you will, the will of God. This act of bringing forth must be evident in the individual's life first and foremost, before translating (when called upon) into prophetic utterances. Secondly, a prophet's authority and security are found in the place of intercession and intimate fellowship with God.

If the prophet's essential task is to declare the Word of God in the here and now (forthtelling), the events in his/her life must be a living expression of God's Word as well. The Apostle Paul coined the expression *living epistles* based on this understanding, but more on that later.

LEAD ('NAHAL)

Now, let us turn our attention to the root of the verb 'to lead.' According to Merriam-Webster online dictionary, *'to lead'* means to show the way, to conduct, or to afford passage to a place[9]. However, as good as this definition is, it does not necessarily capture the heart of God.

Most people think that to lead means to have a vision, and people who follow us to help fulfill our own vision and goals. This is self-centered and it does not reflect God's idea of leadership. Examine any failure in leadership in history, and you will discover that this flawed approach was at its root. Clever vision statements can be crafted to conceal the narcissistic nature of most leaders, but as fruit inspectors we should not be moved by external appearances.

The word of God does say that in the last days people will be, among other things, lovers of themselves, lovers of money and boastful.[10] This generation is widely tagged as the most narcissistic in human history by many researchers[11]. No surprise, as true science will always confirm the word of the God.

In view of this reality, it does not take a rocket scientist to observe that most of what we call leadership in the church and in the world today is rooted in the love of self, the love of money, and in arrogance. So, what is lacking in the definition above and where do we go from here?

God's idea of leadership is primarily rooted in the kind of love that is benevolent in nature, or *agape* love in biblical terms. This is the nature of God, and it speaks of a predisposition, a default setting if you prefer. Therefore, this kind of leadership leaves no room for self-seeking. The verb *"to lead"* is first mentioned in Genesis 33:14. It is the Hebrew word *'nahal'*[12], which speaks of a flowing and going to a watering-place, with the notion of care and protection.

In the account of Genesis 33:14, Esau asks Jacob to follow him to his house in the city of Seir. But Jacob, more concerned with the wellbeing of the feeble ones under his care than with his own agenda, turns down Esau's offer. His selflessness is even more evident as he turns down Esau's offer to leave some of his guards with him.

Some scholars view this as a sign of Jacob's lack of trust towards his brother. I disagree. This encounter took place after Jacob's character transplant from his wrestling with the angel of the Lord, and after making peace with his brother.[13] At this time, Jacob was no longer a usurper, supplanter, or heel-catcher. He was now a Prince with God, one who rules with God.

"Then the man said, "Let me go, for the dawn is breaking." "I will not let you go," Jacob replied, "unless you bless me." The man asked him, "What is your name?" He answered, "Jacob." "No longer will your name be Jacob," the man told him, "but Israel, because you have fought with God and with men and have prevailed." (Genesis 32:22-28 NET)

Prior to this experience with the angel of the Lord, Jacob was always relying on his own strength by tricking his way into breakthroughs. Not anymore: as one who now ruled with God, Jacob's act was selfless. His leadership began to reflect the benevolent, caring, and protective nature of God. He was not suspicious; he was a new man whose actions finally began to reflect the influence of God's leadership in his life.

Perhaps Jacob did not realize this, but through this selfless act, the children were preserved, thus preserving the Seed through which God's purposes were to be accomplished on the earth. From these children came the twelve tribes of Israel and all the successive faith heroes that we have come to admire and love, including the Seed of God, Jesus the Messiah.

This example reflects the heart of the Lord concerning leadership. It is exactly what David meant by our Shepherd leading us beside quiet waters. The quiet waters here not only represent a place of refreshing, but a resting place.[14]

| DIVINE INHERITANCE

The mention of rest in scriptures is often made in parallel with the fulfillment of a promise. Therefore, prophetic leadership aims to bring others to their place of divine fulfillment in Christ. It is not meant to motivate people into serving our own agendas. Instead, it aims to guide the people of God to where He destined them to find the full expression of their divine nature.

From the brief word study above, we can therefore define prophetic leaders as those who are able to *hear what God says and live it out with the fundamental purpose of helping others access their own place of divine inheritance*. With this understanding, it becomes evident that such leaders have always existed at critical moments in history, certainly throughout biblical history. Yet even now, the time is ripe for God to raise up a standard in our generation to counter the agents of darkness that are gaining ground in our societies.

Opposite Forces

| FRICTION

In Physics, Newton's third law teaches us that, "to every action, there is an equal and opposite reaction."[15] In plain language, each time you apply force against an object which is at rest, there is an equal force that the object is applying against you.

Furthermore, this opposing force often exerts itself in the contrary direction of intended motion. Therefore, it has the potential to hinder the object's movement. This is a scientific definition of resistance. This principle is also true in the spirit or unseen realm, which is the origin of everything we physically observe.

In other words, anything that is observable in the physical (seen) realm is simply a manifestation, or materialization if you will, of a spiritual (intangible) reality. Paul the Apostle hinted at this truth when he stated that, "His invisible qualities - both His eternal power and divine nature - have been clearly seen, because they can be understood from what He has made."[16]

You may have heard some people say things like: "you are the sum total of your thoughts." That is because our thoughts exist in the invisible realm, but we can have some level of insight into what men think by looking at their actions. Any action we take in the physical realm is the expression of a thought which was conceived in the intangible realm. If that makes sense, let us therefore consider the spiritual origins of friction.

Ever since the God created the universe, evil has been at work to oppose and undermine His good purposes. God is light, and light naturally shines the brightest amid darkness. According to the book of Genesis, darkness was over the surface of the deep until the Lord said: *"Let there be light."* He did not stop there: He also made sure to create a line of separation between light and darkness.[17]

For God to be the essence of every substance that went on to exist on the earth, it means that darkness had to be removed from the canvas of creation because there is no darkness in Him. This is precisely why scriptures say that "the whole earth is full of His glory."[18]

The direct implication is that light and darkness cannot coexist or simultaneously share the same space. Light has the inherent capacity to keep darkness at bay, and darkness can only rule in the absence of light.

Embedded in the account of creation is the spiritual origin of friction, the first occurrence of two opposite entities wrestling for dominion. In this account, light exercised dominion over darkness, and darkness retreated, and it has been the same outcome ever since.

The presence of darkness always points to the absence of a shining light. This reflects the darkness' inability to contain light where it is administered, as John rightly pointed out: "The light shines in the darkness, and the darkness has not suppressed it."[19]

Yet, the interesting characteristic of darkness is that it is always lurking to seize every opportunity to rule as soon as light departs from the scene. From the beginning, God wanted us to know that there is a spiritual force called darkness that will not miss an opportunity to fill every realm that is not inhabited by light.

| CREATED FROM LIGHT

In the first chapter of John's Gospel, we learn that all things were made through the Word of God and without Him nothing was made that came to existence. Later, the Lord Jesus declared that He is the light of the world and that whoever follows Him will never walk in darkness but will have the light of life.[20]

If we apply the Law of First Mention to the word *light*, we discover that it first appears in God's first recorded words: *Let there be light*. Thus, Light was the foundation upon which all the other works of creation stood.

Before light came, there was no sign of life on the earth. Instead, there was chaos and darkness. Inasmuch as the word light is meant here literally, it is also meant spiritually or in matters of the mind. Some synonyms of the word light are brightness, wisdom, or intelligence.

Prophetically, light often represents truth and revelation. God made nothing apart from wisdom and truth, which are facets of the Spirit of the Lord Jesus Himself, the revealed image of God. The LORD possessed wisdom *in the beginning* of His way, even before His works of old[21], and we know that *in the beginning* was the Word that became flesh.

THE GOODNESS OF LIGHT AND THE PURPOSE OF DARKNESS

God for calls light a good thing. Who can blame Him? In fact, it is the first thing that God ever called good. "God saw that the light was good…"[22] There is something cheerful and pleasant about light. I humbly suggest that people who have never experienced living in darkness for an extended period simply cannot get a full appreciation of light. Let me explain.

Growing up in a third-world country, we were accustomed to lengthy power outages regularly. I am talking about three days out of seven at times, and sometimes more. Many times, I went to bed so afraid that I slept in the same position till morning break, thinking that ghosts would creep in my bed. On a less dramatic note, I can recall the numerous humorous times folks would slam their feet or heads on furniture trying to find their way around a dark room in the middle of the night.

The fear of being burglarized on a dark street, or the times when we struggled with studying because of an unannounced power outage were common. It is hard to imagine what went through many parents' minds on those days. But whenever power would return after several days (or hours), the euphoria could be heard miles away, comparable to a city cheering for a game winning score in a Superbowl.

Times of prolonged darkness certainly gave us a deeper appreciation for light. And the perceived degree of darkness covering the nations of the earth today plays a comparable role: it is creating a platform for those who abide in the Kingdom of Light to shine brighter. Let us rejoice, for it is impossible to go unnoticed at this hour unless we choose to hide. As it says in Isaiah 60:2-3:

> "See, darkness covers the earth and thick darkness is over the peoples, but the LORD rises upon you and his glory appears over you. Nations will come to your light, and kings to the brightness of your dawn."[23]

| NO COEXISTENCE

We saw that light is precious and it is the first thing that God called good. He did not explicitly call darkness evil, yet He made it a point to bring forth life through light *only* and said it was good. If God were fond of darkness, He would have called it good and do the works of creation through it. Instead, He dissociated the works of creation from the darkness.

Light and darkness, life and death, or if you will, good and evil are the two opposite forces that influence the affairs of men and as we saw earlier, they were not meant to provide a thriving environment if mixed together.

Adam introduced both good and evil to his initial state of perfection, and mankind has been fainting ever since. Light is mostly associated with life and abundance, while darkness usually produces a sense of death and emptiness.

It is evident that from the beginning God has been trying to communicate that life and good cannot find their truest meaning outside of the Light, Jesus Christ. It is also easy to see the effect of Satan's trickery on Adam and Eve. He successfully made them believe that they could thrive by mixing light and darkness within them. By eating the tree of the knowledge of good and evil, they effectively became a house divided that could no longer stand.

One of the direct implications of this fundamental error was the corruption of man's leadership purpose. God desired man to exercise dominion over creation. However, the faithful exercise of this mandate was based on man's dependency on the Light as the essence of his leadership ability.

This would have ensured that every man's desire to lead found its expression in establishing others in their own divine expression of rulership over creation. Instead, we have inherited a humanistic type of leadership that seeks to exercise dominion over other men. As Myles Munroe adroitly puts it:

> "Everyone desires to influence because we naturally want to be in control. Yet we've confused influence with domination. According to the original design, we're not supposed to dominate other people but to have dominion over the earth and its resources. When we don't understand this distinction, we manipulate and abuse others and frustrate the expression of their own God-given leadership nature… The true nature of leadership is the attraction of others to our gifts, which are deployed in their service."[24]

| THERE IS HOPE

As we get closer to the restoration of all things, let us be filled with an unshakable hope. The Lord is surely leading us to a city in which there will be no need for the sun or the moon to shine, because the Light of His glory will fill the earth. All forms of darkness (spiritual and physical) will be expelled from the face of the earth, and we will reign with Him forever. Now, that sounds like a victorious declaration to me, Hallelujah![25]

Prophetic leaders develop the ability to discern the activities of good and evil in the sphere(s) of influence they have been called to. However, there is one thing that sets them apart from other leaders and human beings who, because of the fall of mankind, are also able to know good from evil.

They are reunited to the Essence of leadership and governed by God to demonstrate and establish His righteousness on the earth. They are also called to exhort and teach others how to exercise it at their own level. In fact, the apostle Paul, one who modeled the prophetic leadership spirit stated:

> "For you used to be darkness; but now, united with the Lord, you are light. Live like children of light, for the fruit of the light is in every kind of goodness, rightness, and truth – try to determine what will please the Lord. Have nothing to do with the deeds produced by darkness, but instead expose them…This is why it says, 'Get up, sleeper! Arise from the dead, and the Messiah will shine on you!'" (Ephesians 5:8-13, CJB)

We must understand which side of the pendulum we belong to and draw a clear line of demarcation between the two antagonistic forces that are dictating the course of history. This kind of discernment will help us solve problems that would be impossible to solve otherwise. We therefore need to snap out of our delusions of coexisting light and darkness.

The body of Christ has been compromising while playing patty cake for way too long. It is time to arise from our slumber, so the Lord may shine on us and firmly establish us on the right side of history.[26]

History Rhymes

There are no "empty spaces" in the spirit realm because everything is inhabited, either by the light of the Lord or by spiritual darkness. The same is true in the physical world, for the places that we visibly perceive as empty with our natural eyes are still filled with a natural yet invisible matter: air.

This principle is also true in the sphere of leadership. Just as darkness wastes no time invading spaces bereft of light, whenever there is an absence of leadership, it will be quickly filled by someone. If the noble ones do not rule the profane will."[27]

Remember that even within the context of world history, men and women who exemplify prophetic leadership have existed in the past. Although they were not your typical "religious folks," God used them greatly to preserve the seed through which His purposes would be accomplished on the earth.

One of the most illustrious examples of this breed of men was Winston Churchill, a visionary driven by an unwavering sense of divine destiny in his generation. In 1891 at the age of sixteen, he declared to his close friend Murland Evans:

> "... I have a wonderful idea of where I shall be eventually ... I see vast changes coming over now a peaceful world ... London will be attacked, by what means I do not know, but I shall be in command of the defenses of London and will save London and England."

His friend Evans was shocked by that bold statement. He asked Churchill how he could talk like that, and then asked Churchill if he was going to be an army general. Churchill replied that he was not sure. Just like many of us, he knew that he had an important calling, but he did not exactly know how things would unfold.

However, his main objective was clear: he was going to be the one leading England to victory over some sort of evil, although there was no indication of trouble at the time he was awakened to his destiny.[28]

Churchill may not have known that he was indeed a general in the making in the army of God to preserve humanity from the spirit of antichrist that was brooding over Europe long before World War I. Even early in his life, you can see that he was a man who had a real sense of purpose and discernment. He carried a burden for his nation.

That bold statement sure sounded borderline presumptuous for a sixteen-year-old. But if we analyze its content without bias, we can identify striking similarities with the type of statements that were made by some biblical prophets.

Let us be clear! I am not saying that Churchill was a type of biblical prophet. I am simply directing your attention to the fact that his vision, journey, and leadership as a statesman had prophetic overtones that cannot be ignored, as we will see later.

Abraham Heschel described the biblical prophet's word as a scream in the night. While the world is at ease and asleep, the prophet feels the blast from heaven. This blast from heaven is the weight of the burden that is laid upon him, because of his great sensitivity to evil. He begins with a message of doom; he concludes with a message of hope.[29]

This is why many immature believers cannot stand true prophets. They are not interested in what grieves the Father's heart but only what gratifies their flesh. Therefore, they tune out early under conviction, and miss out on receiving true substantial hope and lasting blessing.

Anyway, in Churchill's case, it is evident that his declaration came in a time of relative ease and peace. Yet, he perceived evil waiting at a distance, and concluded with a statement of hope.

Although Churchill was not known as an overtly religious man, he was fundamentally influenced in his youth by his nanny and confidant, who was a passionate woman of prayer. She helped him memorize his first scriptures, knelt with him daily as he recited his prayers, and explained the world to him in distinctively Christian terms.[30]

Privately, he was a devout student of the scriptures, often quoting and paraphrasing Bible passages in his speeches and was able to inspire hope, faith, and strength in the world's darkest hour because of his trust in God's plan.[31]

Most importantly, his biblical insight is what ultimately helped him discern the true nature of Nazism. Churchill wanted no part of it and was repeatedly ridiculed and rejected by his own people for sounding the alarm.

Like an old testament watchman during Israel's times of peace and prosperity, he was a revolutionary who confronted the rise of Nazism and his peers' open reverence of Hitler. He was the only one who called out Nazism for the evil that it was from day one. Thankfully, he saw himself as the providential solution to end it.

It is not until England was at the sudden brink of extinction that they realized that the only one who could lead the "free" world to freedom was the same man they marginalized for *prophesying* these catastrophic events for the previous decades. They did not realize that Churchill's entire life had been a preparation for his crucial role in history.

Yet none of this would be possible if Churchill did not awaken to his purpose, develop discernment by studying scriptures, and set his face like a flint to fulfill what he believed to be his God given destiny.

The wheat and the weeds

One of the famous parables in the New Covenant is the one on the wheat and the weeds, recorded in Matthew 13:24. In summary, Jesus narrates how the kingdom of heaven is like a good man planting good seed in the field. Yet, *while everyone was asleep*, his enemy came in and sowed weeds.

For those with a little bit of agricultural knowledge, weeds are generally viewed as undesirable, or bad plants. In order words, bad seed. The story evolves into the good man's servants wondering how weeds have sprouted among the good seed. Consequently, the good seeds are left to grow with the weeds until the day of harvest because uprooting them too early would also cause the wheat to be destroyed in the process.

This parable is a good illustration of what took place in the garden of Eden. God came and planted an uncorrupted seed in the garden. The good seed was the nature of God, and the garden was the heart of mankind. Then Adam, the garden's watchman, was indifferent while the enemy planted corruption in the heart of Eve, the seed multiplier.

That harvest produced Abel (wheat) and Cain (weed), and we know how that story unfolded. Most people today are like Adam: lulled to sleep and wondering why their lives, families, businesses, ministries, are devastated by wickedness. Arise! We are fast approaching the days of the final harvest. I do not know about you, but I refuse to wake up someday to a harvest that I have not planted.

The enemy is not good at producing anything good or beneficial for humanity. He only comes to kill, steal, and destroy what already exists.[32] Furthermore, he does not have the ability to create, so he resorts to copying and distorting what is already established in order to deceive those who are undiscerning. The Bible even goes as far as to say that he masquerades himself as an angel of light.[33]

| WORLD WAR 2

Let us examine the parable of the wheat and the weeds within the context of World War II. Regardless of our level of appreciation or dislike for Churchill, we can all agree that he had a noble cause at heart: one to defend his fellow countrymen from imminent destruction. His vision and persistence made him a timeless leader.

Since we established earlier that good and evil are always in opposition, Churchill could have only become a hero in history if his accomplishments resulted in defeating some sort of evil. If the enemy can sow evil to counter good according to the Lord Jesus Christ, then it is fair to look at Churchill's direct enemy at the time: Hitler.

In 1905, also at the age of sixteen years old, Hitler attended Rienzi's opera performance with his friend August Kubizek. Rienzi, among other occult influences that shaped Hitler's spirituality, was the messenger that the enemy used to spark his evil agenda. Lucifer was created by God with the primary purpose of worshipping God, but he ended up using his talents to exalt himself.[34] It is no surprise that he still uses music today to corrupt the human soul. Scriptures warn us to not be ignorant of the schemes of the enemy and music is one of his oldest tricks.[35]

Therefore, it is critical to pass the things we hear through a filter, for faith comes by hearing and our hearing is a direct doorway to the soul. As the wisest earthly king to ever live warns in Proverbs 4:23, guard your heart above everything else, because from it is the source of life's consequences.

The heart here refers to the seat of emotions, mind and will. These three items make up the soul, the outer layer of the inner man. The physical body is the housing. Physical senses are the gates through which stimuli enter the soul. The words we allow to pass through the hearing gate have the creative power to produce evil or righteousness from within.

Anyway, at the end of this opera performance, August recalls that Hitler, who suddenly looked possessed, gripped his hand, and spoke to him with an unusual hoarse and raucous voice: "he claimed that his destiny was set and that the spirit that would drive it entered into him."

August further relates that when Hitler began to speak, it is as though he was struck by something strange. This incident was so strange that afterwards, Hitler himself showed astonishment at what had just burst forth from him with such primal force.[36]

Just as Churchill before him, Hitler had found a sense of destiny. Even more astonishing is that just like Churchill, his sense of destiny was also revealed at the age of sixteen. Again, Satan cannot create but he is a good imitator.

In the parable above, we learned that the enemy sowed weeds after the nobleman had sowed good seed. It is quite fitting to see in this case that the enemy sowed evil in the heart of a man (Hitler) sometime after the Lord had sowed a noble purpose in the heart of another one (Churchill). Prophetic leaders are vessels that are chosen by God to confront and expose evil within their sphere of influence.

| THE TIME IS RIPE

Remarkably, we are told in the parable that weeds were sown in the field while everyone was asleep. That sounds a lot like the spiritual and intellectual climates of Europe in the early 1930s, which alarmingly resembles the spiritual and intellectual climates in our present time. Just like Europe in the 1930's, the West is again experiencing apparent times of peace and prosperity, while science and truth are being perverted before our slumbering eyes.

The people belonging to the Evil One are being raised in every realm of society, gaining large followership and remarkable loyalty along the way, while the noble ones are sleeping. I prophesy to the dry bones laying in churches' pews to wake up from their deep slumber. The time is ripe, and because of the general sense of fear that has gripped the nations of the earth, we better believe that they are ready for firm and decisive leadership.

Truly, the tables are set for the nations to either blindly follow the Evil One or to be inspired to follow those led by the Holy Spirit. There will be no middle ground this time because the line of demarcation between the wheat and the tares is being drawn and it is getting clearer than ever. Meanwhile, there is still a window of opportunity for the redemption of many.

The end-time harvest is ripe indeed. To preserve His seed on the earth, God is looking to send out a company of prophetic people who are convinced that they are fashioned in incorruptible Seed, dead to personal ambition, but consumed with the fulfillment of a divine mandate. This is a snapshot of the heart of prophetic leaders, and that can be you.

The Lord's Two-Fold Vision

| SEEING THINGS CLEARLY

Good and evil are always in opposition, whether we choose to acknowledge it or not. Part of the problem that the nations of the earth are facing right now is that the church has been put to sleep.

Some of us have been lulled to sleep by false doctrines that cause us to live in a timid way, while fearfully waiting to go to heaven. Others have the flawed impression that Jesus Christ was a non-confrontational guy with shampooed hair and hands as soft as cotton.

The point is, we may have been greatly misled by a misrepresentation of the Lord's character and leadership. Jesus is the perfect antithesis to evil. He never condones or excuses it, but He hates it with passion.

Make no mistake: He came the first time as a lowly servant and the prophet Isaiah goes as far as portraying Him as a lamb led to the slaughter (Isaiah 53:7, NIV). Yet even as a lamb, zeal for the house of God consumed Jesus, and He still managed to confront evil to the point of flipping the tables of merchants in the temple courts in righteous anger and indignation.[37]

If in His first coming as the Lamb He did noy shy away from confrontation, then we better believe that He is coming again as the Lion to strike the nations and reign until He has put all His enemies under His feet.[38]

It is critical that we understand the dual nature of Christ: He is the lion and the lamb, humble and fierce. He is kind yet can deal with those whom He loves with severity. He is currently raising up mighty people to know His voice. These are the champions whom He will lead to confront evil in all spheres of society with demonstrations of His power like we have not yet seen and bring hope in our times as we approach His return.

Inherent to the call of prophetic leaders is the mandate to bring forth the word and the purposes of the Lord. Therefore, such people will walk without the fear of man and in such a manner that upsets the traditions of men, so that the Lord may rule through their lives by His word alone.

Every single one of us is exposed to various forms of evil daily and we react to these experiences with varying degrees of passion, from consuming zeal to complete indifference. I will expand on this a bit later, but for now I invite you to ask the Father if He created you as a solution to some evil that encroaches on your territory.

But know for certain that according to scriptures, if you claim to walk in the fear of the Lord, then you must also "… hate evil; for the Lord hates pride, arrogance, evil ways, and a perverse speech." [39]

| THE INDIVIDUAL

Three years ago, I had the privilege to sit down for an interview with a senior church leader. I loved what he had to say: "There is such a desperate need for prophetic leadership. Those who can see into the future and can formulate a plan for meeting the future successfully."

There can be no leadership without an ability to see into the future. That is what is commonly referred to as vision. In other words, "To become a leader, you must catch hold of a vision of a future that reflects the fulfillment of your life's purpose."[40] Like Winston Churchill as we saw earlier, we must be able to see into the future and decide what we need to do in preparation for the moment when duty calls upon us.

Someone does not necessarily have to be a born-again Christian to be mightily used by the Lord for a specific task. Some may cringe at that statement. But if God can use a donkey to speak to a stubborn prophet[41], then He can also use the unsaved for his purposes just as He did with King Cyrus. The Lord has historically used a vast number of people who were not your typical Sunday churchgoer to further His agenda on the earth.

The religious spirit in many Christians would no doubt take offence at the statement above but here is the truth. The fact that, at times, God had to rely on a donkey or a "non-Christian" to accomplish certain things is a further indictment for His people.

It speaks to our inability to hear His voice, our unwillingness to obey His voice, or worse our cowardliness in the moment of truth. Heck, donkeys and the "non-religious" may obey God better than most modern Christians because they do not carry years of religious garbage that prevent them from recognizing and obeying the voice of God.

A WARNING TO THE SELF-RIGHTEOUS

When Jesus walked the earth, the Pharisees and the Scribes were custodians of the word of God. It was their duty to make handwritten copies of the scrolls and to teach them to the people of Israel. Yet they could not recognize the Messiah whom they taught about daily when He showed up on the scene!

Jesus' attitude was a slap in the face of the "religious elite" of His time. He diagnosed their blindness to be so severe that He chose instead to build His Kingdom with a bunch of unlearned and unsophisticated people. He is about to do the same in this generation.

Today, we have churchgoers who are much more "educated and sophisticated" than the disciples ever were. They have Bible apps at their fingertips that are not as nearly opened as Instagram. They love to sit down for hours around coffee to criticize ministers, believing that their way of "worshipping" the Lord is the best. But spend enough time around them, and you quickly realize they have no weight in the Spirit and are as dry as a grain of sand in the Saharan desert.

Yes, some of you need to put this book down for a moment and ask the Lord Jesus to deliver you from your sense of religious superiority. Quit comparing yourself (or your church) to others, or you may have a rude awakening when you see the types of people that Jesus anoints for service in the days ahead, while he passes you by! "What has been is what will be, what has been done is what will be done, and there is nothing new under the sun." (Ecclesiastes 1:9, CJB)

INSTEAD, OBEY HIM

There are numerous biblical accounts where the Lord commands nature and it obeys without resistance. Case in point, Jesus once rebuked the storm and it quieted immediately. It is even within the realm of possibilities for rocks to shout out in worship[42] of His majesty if we choose to keep silent.

But to us whom God has granted the ability to make choices, the greatest proof of our love and allegiance to Him is our obedience as Jesus said, "If you love me, you will keep my commands." (John 14:15, CJB)

If we genuinely love Him, we will naturally want to do what He commands us to do. He is longing for His people to stand in the gap, and with the end-time harvest at stake, He will not have use for the cowardly.[43]

If it means using an animal to do the job instead of a lukewarm or spineless believer to complete the task of the hour, then He will do it. If it means to pick someone else to fulfill the purpose that He gave you while on earth, then He will do it. His purposes are eternal, and we are expendable if we choose to camp outside of His will for us.

For instance, Elijah asked God to take his life in fear of Jezebel and ran away from his assignment. After attempting twice to get him back on track, God did not argue with him, and told him to go and anoint Elisha as a prophet in his place. Elijah found Elisha as a farmer (an unlearned). Yet God had chosen him to carry the mantle and finish the job.

Prophetic leadership is driven by what God wants to do, when He wants it done, and how He wants it done. The lives of those who submit to the prophetic leadership process are characterized by a longing to stand in His counsel and abide in the will of God.

The Lord is looking to use the faceless and nameless, like Elisha. He will use the weak things to confound the armies of the wise once again, like Gideon. He will train and send the unlearned and unsophisticated in this generation to accomplish His purposes. He is only asking for those who are willing to embrace the journey of a life laid down in obedience to His guidance.

| THE BODY OF CHRIST

If God can use a donkey or an unsaved person, then how much more can He accomplish through His own people when they hear His voice and obey? The body of Christ has a clear prophetic mandate and should be teaching others how to lead prophetic lives.

We know that leadership requires a vision of the future, and the church has the greatest visionary in history as its Leader. He has given us a glimpse into the future and a clear description of our corporate role throughout scriptures.

Christ is coming back to separate the sheep from the goats and rule over the earth. The church has been given a sure vision of how it all ends. Until then, it is our common purpose to make disciples of all nations and immerse them into the reality of the Kingdom of God.[44]

Many Christians refer to this as the great commission. It sure sounds good during our Sunday sermons and our fun Bible studies. But do we genuinely love the Lord? Have we come to the realization that the time of His return is deeply linked to our level of obedience to this great command? If we really loved Him, wouldn't we burn with an insatiable desire to fulfill His vision?

This corporate mandate, however, will be fulfilled according to God's unique calling for each believer and to the degree to which we can hear His proceeding word. Some of us should no longer rely on mister famous pastor's Sunday soundbites or run like deer in headlights from one conference to another.

There is a time and a season for that, as I have been there myself. But there comes a time when relying on another's relationship with the Lord becomes as good as relying on a dead clock: it will be right twice a day but that is about it.

The church as a body is called to be a prophetic group of people sharing a common purpose. As Jesus once said, "My sheep listen to My voice, I recognize them, they follow me, and I give them eternal life." (John 10:27-28, CJB)

| A PROPHETIC HERITAGE

We often make it too complex for believers to become aware of their prophetic DNA. As a result, many children of God doubt the notion that they are called to be a prophetic people. We have glamourized and commercialized the prophetic so much that many subconsciously think that only certain superstars behind a ministry title can hear the voice of God and communicate it.

The result is that many people seek to be prophets without proper understanding and end up in shipwreck. In other circles, the leadership has placed so many religious yokes on people that they believe that you must be so special to become a prophetic person.

As the Apostle Paul noted not all are prophets, though we are all encouraged to operate in the gift of prophecy[45]. At the most basic level, a prophetic person is simply someone who can hear the voice of the Lord and obey or repeat what they have heard.

For instance, your salvation experience is prophetic in nature. Perhaps you heard (or felt) the call of the Lord to turn from your sins and to follow Him, and you obeyed. That alone qualifies you because it is the Spirit of the Lord Jesus that qualifies us!

But that was just the beginning. You were called to continually hear what God says, live it out and/or speak it out. Doing so gradually sets us apart from the practices of the world and turns us into yielded instruments and mighty weapons in God's hand.

Therefore, Jesus said: "Man shall not live by bread alone, but by every word that proceeds from the mouth of God."[46] In other words, there are dimensions of fulfillment that we will not experience on this earth unless we continue to hear and respond to the voice of God.

| ARE YOU ALIVE TO DEATH, AND DEAD TO LIFE?

This way of living is in stark contrast to the flawed notion of going to church every Sunday, paying the bills, and perpetually trying to build all kinds of safety nets in our lives until we escape to heaven by the skin of our teeth.

Most of us live in a way that screams to the unsaved: "Please do not look here! We are as scared of death and uncertainty as you are!" Yet, there is a clear calling to venture out beyond the realm of salvation, and the purpose of initiating a call is to stimulate a response: will you answer the call?

By His death, Jesus overcame the one who *had* (past tense) power over death (that is, the devil), and as a result He set free those who had been in bondage all their lives because of their fear of death. The devil no longer has power over death!

We must realize that passivity is a choice to remain a slave, alive to death and dead to the life that awaits you in the call of God. However, the kind of response required to propel us into the life that can only be found beyond the reins of fear cannot be triggered if we do not have a sense of divine destiny.

| A SPONTANEOUS EXHORTATION

Perhaps growing up you have always been angered by the absurdly high divorce rates within the church. Perhaps you were a child growing up apart from your parents due to a divorce.

What if the Lord could use the pain that the enemy intended for evil to mold in you a heart of compassion? What if this well of compassion was meant for you to become a voice carrying His authority to bring healing to others experiencing the same? What if the Lord created you to become a counselor to young adults so that by your coaching and shepherding, He may build fruitful marriages following biblical principles?

What if through your obedience many families would produce a generation of righteous children who would grow to occupy every major sphere of influence in society? What if as a result, nations would be led by the righteous and rejoice instead of groaning from the wickedness of current leadership[47]? What if your obedience became a key factor in the Lord's purpose to have the nations as His inheritance?

| YOU ARE A DIVINE SOLUTION

Having a sense of divine destiny moves us to realize that our lives are God's solution to a specific problem. Consequently, every trial leading up to our appointment is a key component in our preparation.

However, there is a trigger event that must take place before a prophetic leader can move from the stage of discovering their purpose to the stage of preparation. Like Joseph, Churchill saw the future prophetically. He believed what he was shown, and he began to act on it.

Not taking initiative is why many people fail to enter the higher calling that they are called to fulfill. Dr. Myles Munroe captured this sad reality in one of his many provocative statements:

> "The wealthiest place on planet earth is the graveyard because there lie books that were never written, evangelistic businesses that were never opened, and a myriad of other types of divine assignments that never saw the light due to the church's lack of courage and misconception of leadership and ministry."[48]

True courage is the confidence that as we engage and continue to partner with God who is the author of our destiny, we cannot fail because His word never fails. Some may argue that Joseph was foolish to share his dream with his brothers and that may very well be true. Yet, a leader must be willing to share his inspiration with others.

There is no doubt Joseph was divinely inspired. He did not do wrong to share his inspiration, he only chose the wrong crowd. Regardless, he believed in God and God remained faithful to fulfill His promise.

Saying nothing would have been the equivalent of shying from the vision for fear of death at the hands of his jealous brothers. If he remained quiet in fear, his entire family and generation would have died of famine. He would have died of famine as well, although he was the divine solution to the famine. The inscription on his grave would have read: "Joseph: God's solution to the world's famine, he feared death, then died of famine." How ironic.

Discover the vision, engage it, and trust God for its fulfilment. God is only bound by His own word. If He is the author of our destiny, then He will fulfill it if we say yes and engage it.

Myles Munroe also exhorted, "God has given you a special purpose to fulfill, but do you know what it is?".[49] If you do, take a moment to invite the light of God to shine on you and consider the prophetic utterances that have been spoken over the course of your life: how many cobwebs would you have to go through before you can accurately recall and articulate each one? Furthermore, can you declare it in a way that convinces you first of your own life's significance to your generation and secondly, compels me to believe it with you? Lastly, what steps have you taken in faith to engage with your divine destiny?

THE STAKES ARE HIGH

Reformation begins with a sense of divine purpose, a purpose that coerces you to believe that humanity would be at a great loss if you did not fulfill your God given destiny. Everyone who has changed history had this prophetic awareness of the calling. They were also aware that the stakes were high: Jesus was an expert carpenter who knew His death was the only way to redeem mankind. Joseph died to the comforts of a loving father's favor and turned into a statesman who changed biblical history in critical times.

Likewise, in more recent history, Churchill knew he was the one to lead England's armed forces to victory over the forces of evil. He was born in a noble family, yet he forfeited the comfort and luxurious living that his parents could afford him. He went through years of rejection, near death experiences and isolation, before becoming the legendary deliverer of the free world.

What is the battlefield that you have been assigned to? What are the comforts of life that you have forfeited for the sake of the high calling on your life? As we will further see, there is a price to pay because death must be wrought in us for His glory to be released through us.

You see, warfare is not limited to the military, and it never was. The current events on earth are physical manifestations of the wrestling taking place between light and darkness in the invisible realm. It is obvious that the forces of darkness have been using schools, churches, homes, businesses, governments, hospitals, etc. as tools to impose an evil dominance over mankind.

| AWAKE, SLEEPY CHAMPION

Your educational, professional, or life background was not just so you could be defined by a job title (or status) or a steady income. Thank God for paychecks but if that is all Jesus died for then He failed miserably. I know He did not fail, so where does that leave us?

I am sensitive to those who have a background that the enemy meant to use for evil. I want to encourage you that the Lord can redeem it in your preparation for the kind of leadership that the world so desperately needs. The times call for benchwarmers to become key players in the greatest move of God yet on the earth.

There is a sleepy champion within you waiting to be strategically released to the harvest field and bring the spoils of victory home. Warfare might be raging all around us, but Jesus already overcame the world. Yet, these prophetic champions must rise and take the Kingdom by force so His victory can be established in the hearts of men, once and for all.

Zeal without knowledge can be dangerous. Man will always experience unrest while living outside of the call of God for their lives. At times during the process of becoming, things may look as though we have missed the call of God, and that can sometimes be discouraging.

For that reason, it is important to explore some of the key principles that God uses to prepare a prophetic leader. To do so in a way that can bring a tangible impartation to you, I will heavily use personal testimonies backed with biblical references in the next section.

PART TWO

THE MAKING OF A PROPHETIC LEADER

Separating Identity from Familiarity

| THE LIMITATIONS OF A FAMILY NAME.

Every man or woman was designed by God to start their earthly journey as newborns, and experience successive stages of growth. Each stage is characterized by distinct marks of physical, psychological, and mental transformations as the individual continues to grow.

Similarly, when an individual is born again into the Kingdom of God, they become a new creature through the supernatural experience of the new birth. To this effect, Jesus told one of the Pharisees, Nicodemus: "Unless a person is born again from above, he cannot see the Kingdom of God."[50].

There are also stages of spiritual transfiguration, or maturing if you will, that take place in the life of each believer. At each stage, our roles and responsibilities also evolve as we grow spiritually.

Now, every person is usually given a name at birth. In most cultures, individuals receive at least two names. A unique name or first name, and a family name which is typically meant to convey the person's belonging to a specific family or tribe. In Jesus' time for instance, it was common to see someone mentioned as "Simon, son of Jonah" to differentiate them from others carrying the name Simon.

Naturally, it is easy to understand why humans tend to develop a sense of pride that makes them want to honor their family name. However, God causes certain events to take place in the lives of those with great prophetic destiny to suppress this natural, although noble human ambition.

This is one of the reasons why there was no use of last names in the Bible. The characters were primarily known by their first names. It is as though God deliberately omitted them. Think about it. God does nothing by accident, and we better believe that there is a good reason for this as well. Regardless of His motive, it is evident that God preferred identifying His people primarily through their own given (first) name.

| WEANING

A fundamental part of the training in the life of a prophetic leader (or anyone called to lead a prophetic life), will often involve the Lord orchestrating a form of separation from family and/or familiarity. This may be for a season or permanently, depending on the kind of process that He believes is best suited for your unique makeup, and the specificity of His call on your life.

For instance, it did not take long before I realized that drawing my identity from my family was not as strong of a foundation. Growing up in my parents' home I always felt and acted differently than the other kids in the neighborhood, but I still drew my sense of identity from my family heritage. I was more than blessed to have caring and upright parents.

They were my heroes, and I knew that I meant the world to them. They taught me generosity, respect for self and others, integrity, and the importance of a good education. My father had been a professor for many years before becoming a Medical Representative for a multinational, and my mother was a Judicial Officer. As you can imagine, there was a great deal of instruction, discipline, and order in the house. However, the Lord has a way of weaning people off their sources of comfort when it is time to prepare them for prophetic destiny.

One of those sources of comfort is the sense of identity drawn from our earthly families. In December 2004 at the ripe age of seventeen, I left my home, everything, and everyone that I knew to attend university in the Unites States, or so I thought at the time. It did not help that I left ninety-degree weather and landed in a giant freezer with blocks of ice climbing to the housetops.

This giant freezer was named Minnesota, the land of ten thousand lake-size ice cubes as I call it. To me, the sunlight felt no different than the imitation of a refrigerator's light. It was a baptism of fire like no other. Without my knowledge, the Lord had enrolled me in His school of the prophets.

| ABRAHAM

Abraham was a multigenerational example of the biblical prophetic leader. To help put this into proper perspective, Abraham's fatherhood is currently claimed by the Jews, Muslims, and Christians all around the world today. According to the Pew Research Center, these three groups make up over 55% of the earth's population.[51]

One can factually argue that Abraham has a larger following (in today's social media lingo) than Jesus Himself, and they would be right. Of course, we are strictly comparing numbers to numbers here and not their lives impact in view of eternity, as we know Jesus gets the nod on the latter.

So, speaking of prophetic leaders, we must pause and examine Abraham's life especially since he was the first person recorded in the Bible to be called a *prophet* by God Himself. We are not saying Abraham was the first biblical prophet; that would be Abel. But staying true to the Law of First Mention, we are focusing on the first time the word *prophet* is introduced in scriptures.

The prophet Moses (another prophetic leader in history) begins the biblical account of Abraham's life in the book of Genesis, chapter twelve. He gives the reader a radical and abrupt encounter. Up to this point, nothing is known of Abraham, and the first time he is mentioned God tells him to leave his entire father's household, his country and all his kinsmen to some unknown land.[52]

Abraham did well to obey the voice of God, but he made the slight mistake of taking his nephew Lot with him. It is hard to blame him; imagine moving to an unknown land all alone with little to no preparation. What is fascinating is that God did not reveal the fullness of His plan to Abraham until he was completely separated from everyone in his family, including Lot.

| THE VEILS OF FAMILIARITY

For as long as Lot was with him, Abraham did not get to fully experience the breath, the length, and the fullness of what was promised to him.[53] This seems like a trivial coincidence, until you realize that in Hebrew the name *"Lot"* means *"veil."* That is right: Lot's presence was the veil keeping Abraham away from a full revelation of his divine destiny. God had commanded him to be completely separated from every family member, and for as long as Abraham's obedience remained incomplete, he was going to experience strife in his place of blessing.[54]

God will lovingly separate prophetic leaders from the things in which they draw a sense of identity. This is important because they are called to challenge the traditions of men and the status quo in their generation. But it is impossible to do so if they are still manipulatable by cultural and family ties. This sovereign act of weaning may happen at various stages during the journey, as He moves us from one stage of maturity to another.

What is (are) the veil(s) of familiarity and tradition that you are still trying to drag along with you into the destiny that God is trying to separate you unto? Take a moment to pause and ask the Lord to reveal the people, things, and places from which you are still drawing a sense of identity from. Then ask Him to separate you from the ones that are dimming your ability to see a greater revelation of His plans for you.

| DIVINE INTERRUPTION

The Lord separates prophetic leaders from the familiar to mentor them. He orchestrates the events in the life of such individuals to separate them to Himself and/or His intended purposes. For the ones who do not qualify as prophets in the biblical sense, He does it so that they must at least learn to see the world through the lenses of His Spirit. Without it, we cannot be used effectively as His agents to partner with His agenda on the earth.

Sandys captured this reality in the life of Churchill: "Were it not for events fifty years later, young Winston's prediction might be dismissed as the desperate effort of a *lonely* adolescent with a need for affirmation…"[55] In his time, it was common and almost a rite of passage for children born in upper-class families to experience detachment from their parents.

In Churchill's case, his parents were physically and emotionally removed from his life while he attended a distant boarding school. But it was a blessing in disguise because that is how his nanny became his confidant and best friend, and the one who helped frame his worldview through scriptures.

Again, although I am not accusing Churchill of being a prophet or a man of God in any way, it is undeniable that God was prophetically involved in his training early on. He was estranged from his parents (his familial source of identity) yet the only source of love and care that he received for eleven years as a young boy was from a non-relative that God strategically placed in his life to give him a biblical worldview – his prayerful nanny.

He had lost touch with the comforts of home, and the Lord used his isolation to build the scriptural foundation he was going to need several years later. It paid off, as his biblical insight is what ultimately helped him discern the true nature of Nazism from day one. Meanwhile, his peers and colleagues were falling under the spell of Hitler's seductive tactics.

Prophetic people are inevitably led to a place in which God becomes the One from whom they must draw their identity. Once I arrived in the United States in that faithful winter of 2004, my natural source of identity was no longer at arm's length. I am no Churchill and certainly no Abraham but in a comparable way, I was physically separated from anything and anyone that gave me a sense of identity and comfort.

Efforts to preserve the family name's honor became pointless as a stranger in a new land. I was a sensitive teenager gifted with a highly analytical and inquisitive mind, who longed to be mentored by my earthly father. Like Churchill, mine was far away.

Like Abraham, I was in a completely different land than his. It would have been unfair to my father to expect anything more than what he had already done. We were in diametrically opposing worlds, and I needed to adapt fast. Meanwhile, life did not wait for me to blossom before handing me all kinds of blows and challenges that were ushered by a near-death experience and a painful betrayal that forever altered the course of my existence.

| NEAR-DEATH EXPERIENCE

The late R. Loren Sandford, one of my prophetic fathers in the faith wrote:

> "It is not unusual for a prophetic type – or anyone with a high calling – to have been born in the midst of some kind of life-threatening trauma or to have a history of scrapes with death or serious injury. The enemy of our soul has an obvious vested interest in cutting off a destiny before it can happen, especially when that destiny touches the lives of many. Pharaoh sought to kill all the male babies in Israel in order to reduce the threat their numbers represented. Moses' family saved his life by placing him in a basket and floating him downriver, where Pharaoh's daughter found him and raised him as her own. Jesus was born under similar circumstances. Herod tried desperately to kill Jesus before He could reach the age of two."[56]

One such incident took place in my life in the winter of 2006. I was involved in a terrible traffic accident which by all accounts was a miraculous escape. While driving on the interstate's left-most lane on my way to work on an early Saturday morning, I felt something hit the right rear side of the vehicle. The hit came with such force that it sent the Jeep Cherokee spinning to the left and coming straight at the median. I sure thought that was the end.

Right before impact, a picture of my mother followed by a picture of Jesus flashed before my eyes and things went dark for a moment. When I came back to my senses and visibly shaken, people were risking their own lives by running across the snowy freeway from the right-most lane and rushing towards my vehicle.

They were all in complete shock to see me alive and I did not know why until I stepped out of the car. I then realized that not only was the vehicle completely totaled but the airbags did not even blow up! I came out without a scratch or limp, and the sturdy SUV was completely smashed.

Bystanders reported that the car had violently hit the median, front facing, at full impact twice while it spun and that I should have been at least dealing with a neck injury at best. Amazingly, there was a big dent on the right tail where I thought I had felt impact. Yet, all witnesses reported no car physically hitting me in the rear.

How can that be? In recalling one of his own life-threatening experiences, R. Loren Sandford continued: "Prophetic people need to be covered in prayers from those who love them. Lives and destinies are at stake in an ongoing war."[57] You can bet the forces of darkness in the spiritual realm were looking to abort my destiny, and my mother's prayers saved me!

This event triggered a gut-wrenching betrayal from my guardians that ensued within the same hour. However, unlike Churchill I did not have someone to give me godly counsel at the time. Unlike Abraham, I was not versed in the dealings of God, therefore I could not discern His will in this chaos.

The forces of darkness recognize the call on the lives of those with prophetic destiny at an early age, and they do not wait for us to realize it before seeking to terminate us. The enemy is the *abortioner-in-chief*. He is frantically committed to aborting great prophetic destinies because he dreads the great Light that they carry and its impact on a generation.

Darkness is always lurking, seeking for the slightest diminishing of light to overtake an environment. Wherever light is absent, darkness rules. Another form of darkness is ignorance, and the enemy seeks to capitalize on our ignorance more than we realize. It takes the direct mentoring of God or godly mentoring through a seasoned prophetic person to help us navigate these crucial moments.

| IDENTITY CRISIS

The prophetic leadership process will inevitably cause these champions in-the-making to experience certain events that have the potential to alter the course of their lives. These can often happen in addition to the sense of loneliness they are already experiencing. The way they handle these dealings will either cause them to drink from the lake of bitterness or draw near to the Lord so He can lead them to discover the rivers of living water.

How they deal with loneliness, Sandford states, will determine the shape of their lives, whether it becomes a hard walk of bitterness in isolation and self-protection or a place of deep, sweet, and private communion with God that becomes a fountainhead of peace and love for the sake of others. They may fluctuate between two extremes until they settle on one side or the other.[58]

| MOSES

Moses was separated from his family early on. He experienced an identity crisis during his forty-year training before awakening to the call on his life. Firstly, he miraculously survived a mass murder as a baby. Let us give him that badge of honor right off the bat. Then, he grew up in Pharaoh's palace and received the training and education that would have made him the next king of Egypt.

The man was born a Hebrew slave yet was raised as an Egyptian king. He undoubtedly wrestled with his identity, to the point of murdering an Egyptian soldier in defense of a Hebrew slave. Thinking that would earn him favor in the eyes of his own people, they ended up rejecting him and the Egyptians were out to kill him once again. He then fled in isolation to the back of the desert in deep soul searching.

This took such a toll on him that the Moses we rediscover during his encounter with the burning bush is nothing like the brave man of old. Here is a man who learned the art of diplomatic speech, bravery, assertiveness, and all the attributes necessary to be the ruler of the world's most powerful empire. Yet the betrayal and death threats upon his life led him to a long season of isolation and doubt, so much that a hesitant spirit had now swallowed up his confidence.

| BETRAYAL AND REJECTION

This was certainly true in my own life. Firstly, I escaped death from the womb because my mother refused to abort me despite a very complicated pregnancy, with doctors and my own biological father suggesting her to do so to end her misery. In her own words: "I knew God did not want me to end the life of this baby." I ended up being the only child she could have, due to the medical complications she experienced at my birth. There was the *abortioner-in-chief* at work again, looking to abort God's call on my life before I could see the sun light!

Secondly, the near-death experience and betrayal that I experienced later led me into seven years of uncertainty and confusion. During those years, friends, and family - for no fault of their own - could not provide me with adequate answers. I felt misunderstood by everyone.

To make matters more complicated I did not understand my own self, which made it difficult to communicate my experience with others without the fear of rejection and ridicule. As a result, I grew bitter, frustrated, and emotionally isolated. I longed for love, yet a world of perpetual selfishness surrounded me. Life had lost its meaning. It felt like I had lost the meaning of life even before I could discover it.

If you are reading this book, you were likely separated – or felt a strange urge to be separated - from family or the familiar. If not, you have most likely experienced isolation, rejection, misunderstandings, life-threatening events, and even painful betrayal from the ones that you look up to. Perhaps you are currently experiencing an identity crisis as a result.

Would you put this book down for a moment right now, and ask Jesus to reveal Himself and His will in the midst of your inner turmoil?

BROKENNESS

| THIRST

Human beings often try to find the meaning of life by seeking to gain their identity through a relationship with the world around them. It makes sense, because every activity of man is a result of his attempt to find his identity and purpose. The problem is, we cannot know who we truly are by relating to creation, because creation is not our source – The Creator is.[59]

Dr. Myles Munroe argues that just like a product can never serve its creative purpose outside of its manufacturer's original intent, man cannot truly discover the true purpose for his existence apart from God the Creator. In other words, seeking to quench our thirst for fulfilment apart from the Lifeline that comes from our Creator is nothing but a life experiment that keeps us thirstier and more desperate.

| THE THIRSTY SAMARITAN

Perhaps the best illustration of this truth is found in the fourth chapter of the Gospel of John. As Jesus passed through Samaria,

He came to a town called Sychar, and decided to rest beside Jacob's well around noon. Then, a Samaritan woman came to draw water from it. The location and the timing of this encounter is incredibly significant. In ancient Israel, it was customary of young women to draw water from the wells for their daily household supply.

However, the first mention of this kind of activity is in Genesis 24:11. In this scene, Abraham's servant (Eliezer) was on a mission to find a bride for Isaac. As he journeyed, he made his camels "kneel down by the well outside the city. It was evening, *the* time when the women would go out to draw water." [60]

The Bible explicitly indicates that the apportioned time dedicated to this activity was *evening*. So clearly, the Samaritan woman's choice to draw water at noon instead of evening was out of the ordinary.

It gets better. According to ancient customs, wells were also commonly known as betrothal scenes. As Julye Bidmead describes:

> "As the young women likely went out together to collect water, young men of the village realized that this event gave them a perfect opportunity to socialize with the women away from the watchful eyes of the girls' fathers and male relatives. The Hebrew Bible recounts several women meeting their future spouses at wells. The narratives follow a similar literary pattern: A man travels to a foreign land, where he meets a young woman who draws water for him. After meeting with the girl's family, a marriage is arranged." [61]

Evidently, this was common practice, especially when we consider that the future brides of Isaac, Jacob, and Moses – just to name a few – were all met at a well. Strikingly, Jesus is also traveling to a foreign land (Samaria), where He meets a young woman and asks her to draw water for Him. The only problem is that this was not the normal time for a woman to draw water from the well, and we will soon discover why.

Jesus engaged the woman in a conversation, but she was at first hesitant given the hostility between Jews and Samaritans. But Jesus went on to tell her that anyone who drinks from Jacob's well will never be satisfied. He then revealed that if she knew who He was, she would have asked Him for water instead and He would have given her the kind of water that would forever quench her thirst.

However, when she asked Jesus to give her this fountain of water to quench her thirst for good, He said something strange: "Go call your husband and come back here." It turned out, not only she was not married to the man she currently lived with, but she had been divorced five times![62]

In biblical times, it was extremely shameful for a woman to be put away by her husband. This woman had been divorced by her husband five times, so one can only imagine the level of shame she experienced in the community daily. This explains why she chose to draw water at noon, in *isolation*, instead of suffering public humiliation in the evening among the crowd of young adults.

Moreover, water sources were also a common place for divine revelation throughout scriptures. It is only fitting that Jesus addressed her thirst for fulfillment at Jacob's well. Meanwhile, "Jacob" in the

Hebrew language means *"supplanter"*[63]. A supplanter is someone who takes the place of another through scheming or cunning.

| THE SOURCE MATTERS

Our thirst for God is the reason we seek to find fulfillment through our relationship with the world around us. But when it comes to significance, any source that we draw from other than the Creator is a *supplanter* that will perpetually keep us wanting. The Samaritan woman had been jumping from one husband to another in her quest for fulfillment.

Likewise, the prodigal son thought he would find fulfillment through his inheritance (material possessions) and fell flat on his face. Judas Iscariot thought he could find fulfillment by forming an alliance with the religious establishment, and he self-destructed. Adam thought he could find fulfillment within his own ability, and death followed. Just like the characters above - and perhaps you - I were searching for fulfillment, but I was drawing from the wrong wells.

What does it look like in your own life? What are the things – or people - in the wide inventory of creation that have supplanted Christ in your heart's cry for significance? It does not matter if one grew up in church or not.

It is very possible for people to engage in religious activities yet never experience a genuine connection with the Creator. For example, the Pharisees were not only experts in practicing religious rituals, but they were also custodians of the scriptures. Yet when Jesus, the One Whom the same scriptures talked about stood before them, they did not recognize Him and instead wanted to kill Him. Are you finding fulfillment in the Creator or in His creation (people, material goods, or places)?

| ROCK BOTTOM

Hitting rock bottom at some point in life is a common experience among people who follow Jesus in general. This is especially true in the lives of those that have an important prophetic destiny. This sometimes happens because prophetic leaders must come to the place of brokenness and surrender if they are to carry out God's purposes in a way that reflects His character.

To illustrate: young Joseph could surely relate to this. God revealed his future greatness as a ruler in a dream. The next day, in his youthful immaturity, he began to boast about the special call of God on his life to his brothers and father. That attitude further stirred his brothers' jealousy, and they plotted to do away with him.

As the story goes, there was a mighty ruler contemplating *shattered* dreams of greatness while sitting (literally) on rocky ground at the bottom of a pit. He went on to be sold as a slave, then unjustly put in prison for years before the time appointed by God to elevate him as ruler over Egypt.

What about father Abraham? In his days, barrenness brought ultimate shame to a woman. So much that women would sometimes preferred death to the idea of not having a child. Sarah was not only barren, but she was way past the biological age to bear children. Talking about silly hope, no wonder she laughed in unbelief when God promised a son to Abraham.

MY ROCK-BOTTOM EXPERIENCE

The car wreck and betrayal that I experienced in 2006 produced bitterness in my heart and led me to an identity crisis. I began to give into pornography and fornication as I longed for affection. The woman at the well is not an anomaly: at some point we may have tried to satisfy our thirst with things other than the presence of God.

That kind of lifestyle was normal for those around me, having no godly counsel in my life at the time. It did not help that it was a struggle keeping up with bills on my own, so I found myself living with a group of guys who were on average at least ten years older than me.

Nonetheless I managed to get an associate degree within three years of my coming to the United States, and in 2008 I decided to move up north to live near the University in search of greener pastures.

It was a new beginning. Naturally, I sought to fulfill my sense of belonging through new friends. They almost instantly became family because they were much closer to me in age, so I felt I could share life, or whatever I had left to offer without shame or reproach. At the same time, I unfortunately closed off to everyone else.

THE HIDDEN BLESSING OF BROKENNESS

At times, brokenness is what helps us realize that our deepest need is to be reconciled to God. At other times, brokenness is necessary for us to recognize that our second most important need in life is to seek His will for our lives. In my case, it was all the above.

One of the hidden blessings of brokenness is the wooing of the Lord. The enemy uses brokenness to crush our spirits by attempting to lure us further away from our Source, one mirage after another. What he does not want us to know however, is that God can use brokenness to call us back to Him so we can be restored – along with our purpose. But most of us miss it greatly due to pride or lack of understanding.

In his book *Understanding Prophetic People*, R. Loren Sandford talks in great length about the necessity of wilderness sojourns. In his opening statements on the subject matter, he writes: "In the days to come a new generation of leadership will emerge, one trained in hiddenness and purified in the crucible of brokenness."[64]

Properly handling brokenness is crucial in the life of the budding prophetic leader. As Sandford says, wholeness and humility will be the hallmark of the leaders that will soon emerge on the face of the earth.

Brokenness attracts God because it is meant to work humility in us. This is important because without humility we cannot have access to the grace of God. As it is written: "God resists the proud but gives grace to the humble."[65] Furthermore, we can only come to Him by grace. Brokenness is meant to produce in us the key trait that attracts the grace of God in our lives. That key is humility.

| THE DANGER OF REBELLION

Unfortunately, when misunderstood, brokenness can produce the exact opposite of what the Lord desires to produce out of it. Indeed, suffering often magnifies temptation, increasing the opportunity for error. In times like these, Loren Sandford writes:

> "some of us become vulnerable to various forms of immorality in which we indulge simply for the sake of rebellion. *You haven't satisfied me, Lord, so I'll just go look at some pornography! At least there I can feel something!* I often thought. Why can't I just get roaring drunk like anybody else?"

In Loren's case, he knew better not to venture into such activities. Therefore, it is important to disciple our children at an early age, and for them to remain in an environment favorable to the presence of God. Where His presence is, the spirit of holiness and the fear of the Lord are also likely to be present.

While I was home, my mother always insisted that I preserve myself for marriage. Despite flirting with girls as a teenager before leaving my parents' house, I never crossed the line and always refrained from sexual intercourse even when it was offered to me on a silver platter. It even earned me some mocking by my high school peers at the time, but it did not matter. Every time I came near, great fear would grip my heart and I would stop.

But it only takes so much for us to become numb to temptation the more we are exposed to it without godly counsel. Truly, as the Apostle Paul wrote: "bad company corrupts good character"[66], not the other way around.

MY REBELLIOUS YEARS

My experiment in the United States had been one of misfortune from day one, literally. Within eighteen months, I went from having hopes of a bright scholarly future to experiencing betrayal from my guardians right after a near-death experience, working three jobs just to pay the bills while going to college full-time, and dealing with constant pressure, misunderstanding and unfair comparisons from my family members. My self-confidence took a shot because my academic performance was much below what I knew my potential to be.

Suffering has the potential to magnify temptation and it takes strong character to withstand it. The enemy is always seeking whom to devour, and he does not miss an opportunity to approach us in our greatest moments of weakness. For instance, Jesus was in the wilderness for forty days. Satan could have tempted Him on any of those thirty-nine days. But he waited until Jesus's body suffered the deadly pinch of famine to lure Him into sin.

Growing bitter and dejected, I went on to waste many years of my youth in drunkenness, drugs, fornication, and other futilities. This lasted seven years. Engaging in those activities provided an escape from my inner turmoil. The truth is, I was angry at God for all the misfortunes in my life and the fact that no one seemed to understand me. I had been beaten up by life early on for no fault of my own, and my once high moral character was worn out by repeated blows. I was wide open for the enemy's knockout punch.

In 2012, when it seemed that I had found favor with a good job in Silicon Valley, I suffered yet another inexplicable injustice which served as the final straw. Finally in the summer of 2013, I came near the point of surrender.

So, against all hope I applied for a master's degree. My parents could no longer financially support my education the way they once did. They had given it their all and I did not fault them. I loved them, admired their sacrifice, and I wanted to right the ship by betting on my intellectual potential this time.

My friends were settling, others were moving on to new things, and others were simply having a fun time. Meanwhile, I was living in a dear friend's basement. Although their hospitality was one of the kindest, I wanted to respect their privacy and not add to their burden. The Lord needed me to go on an exodus to meet Him, but I could not yet see it.

| INCOMPLETE OBEDIENCE

Earlier we saw how God did not reveal the fullness of His promise to Abraham until Lot, his last family member was removed from his midst. In other words, Lot was the *veil* that kept Abraham from experiencing the full dimensions of his blessing. This is because Abraham had not fully obeyed the command given to him. Obedience is always better than sacrifice, and I too was about to learn that lesson.

As I contemplated moving out of my friend's house, I had a gut feeling that I was supposed to live alone. I had never felt an urge so strong to live alone. Yet, when one of my former roommates asked to join me, I inexplicably gave in. That was a monumental mistake that I came to regret within a couple of weeks. Then, when challenging times came, he went on spending the summer in Canada with his relatives.

The scene depicted the kind of environment the Lord loves to use to speak to us: loneliness, helplessness, and no source of comfort. It is in these moments, when every noise is suppressed, and opportunities to "get busy" are nonexistent, that we can be the most susceptible to humble ourselves and attract His grace.

The Lord's small still voice is difficult to detect in the midst of busyness and much activity. That is why He commands us to "be still" in order to know that He is God. The Lord will reveal Himself to us on His terms, not ours. The sooner we can yield to His desire, the sooner we will get that life-changing encounter.

| BROKENNESS FINALLY ATTRACTS GOD

Brokenness works out humility in our hearts. As I mentioned earlier, humility is a magnet that attracts the grace of God. This is crucial because without grace no man can come to the Lord.

The parable of the prodigal son is a fitting example here. The young man left his father's house in pride, believing that he could make it in life by his inheritance alone. Lacking wisdom, he squandered all his property in reckless living. Relegated to feeding pigs, his ego took a shot. Instead of further rebelling, he finally humbled himself and returned to his source.[67]

Unbeknownst to me, after *seven* years of trying to get my attention, the Lord had *completed* the cycle of breaking through my will and preparing my heart to return to Him. On a certain day during that faithful summer, a friend asked me if I was willing to assist an acquaintance with a job application.

I had heard negative reports circulating around town about this man, including having a recent felony among other issues, and I did not know him. Yet, at that moment I agreed because I felt no better than him. In the past I would have probably acted in self-preservation. But the Lord had finally worked out just enough humility in my heart to come through.

Here is a valuable lesson to learn from this. God will often hide the key to your breakthrough in your willingness to being the key to someone else's breakthrough. This is especially true during seasons of hurt and suffering, so be willing to offer your talents to bless others in tough times!

I agreed to help the man, but little did I know that I was the one truly needing help, and the Lord had sent him to rescue me. My redemption hinged on my willingness to help somebody get the breakthrough they needed, while having no answers for my own troubles. This is so important that I must repeat it. Let us be willing to serve our gifts to those in need, especially during seasons of deep suffering.

Serving others with our gifts has the potential to open doors and bring us into the presence of the great.[68] In my case, the only gifts that I could offer were intangibles (my time and intellect). Unbeknownst to me, the willingness to humbly serve someone else in need with my talents ushered me into the presence of the Greatest.

| DITCH YOUR PRECONCEIVED IDEAS!

Many of us expect God to come to us in spectacular fashion. Many more of us have a preconceived idea of what Jesus or His messengers must look like. As a result, we can easily miss the hour of our visitation, especially if pride clouds our judgement.

In the twenty-fifth chapter of Matthew's gospel, Jesus gives some insight to His disciples on an important discourse that will take place at His return. He reveals one of the factors that will differentiate those who receive eternal life from those who end up in eternal judgement.

> "Then the King will say to those on his right, 'Come, you whom my Father has blessed, take your inheritance, the Kingdom prepared for you from the founding of the world. For I was hungry and you gave me food, I was thirsty and you gave me something to drink, I was a stranger and you made me your guest, I needed clothes and you provided them, I was sick and you took care of me, I was in prison and you visited me… Yes! I tell you that whenever you refused to do it for the least important of these people, you refused to do it for me! They will go off to ternal punishment, but those who have done what God wants will go to eternal life.'"[69]

Because our physical senses are far more developed than our spiritual ones – for most people and Christians in particular, Jesus will often attempt to reveal Himself to men through physical means. And only if we receive Him in that form, will the spiritual dimension be activated as well.

I was asked to bring a stranger to my home, and someone who had been in prison for a felony. Yes, my redemption hinged on my willingness to receive a stranger and felon as a guest, and to help him get a breakthrough.

Quit being upset because you have not seen a winged angel, a burning bush, or some supernova activity in your prayer time. Look around instead at what He places in front of you! Most of us cannot even receive Him in the natural realm, yet we like to pretend that we can discern Him in the spiritual.

God will always act in agreement with the *full* counsel of the written Word. At times, the natural will come first and then the spiritual. In some cases, He might choose sovereignly to come the first time in a display of power. We must be sensitive and receptive to both.

Shortly upon arriving at my apartment this man noticed that I was visibly downcast, and he was determined to know about it before we attended to his own needs. So, I hesitantly shared, and he listened intently without a word.

He proceeded to share his testimony with me – how he came to believe in Jesus while in prison, and I will never forget his last words: "You are a good guy. As far as I know, you have always been out of trouble and respectful towards others. You are smart and good looking. But if you have tried everything *in your own power* to be good and this is where it has led you, why don't you give Jesus a chance?" Afterwards, he handed me his Bible and left.

NONE IS GOOD

Working hard in our own strength to build and preserve a good name before men is a useless endeavor. This is the most fundamental lesson that we must learn sooner than later if we are to be used by God in a powerful way. So, why wait? Until we make peace with that reality and humble ourselves before Him, we will keep running in circles. I was known by most people in town as a good guy, but I was tragically headed to hell like many other "good" people out there who do not come to know the Lord.

Surely, no one can come to the Father except by grace through faith in Christ Jesus.[70] And in Jesus' own words, "None is good but God," and apart from God we can do no good. That is also valid for Christians! We have no reputation, except that of the cross.

HUMILITY AND GODLY LEADERSHIP

The call to prophetic leadership is not just for those who have already experienced the gift of salvation through Jesus Christ. God has a purpose for every human being because He created each human with a gift, talent, or strength. But we must be reconnected to Him if we want to know who we were truly meant to be and what we were meant to do here on earth.

The original mandate was given to mankind to have dominion over the earth. It was meant to be fulfilled by each man serving their gift to fellow human, in subduing the material resources of the earth. Therefore, God's model of leadership was to make every man a servant to others, not lording over them.

The wrong exercise of leadership by dominating over fellow human beings as we see today is not a new thing. A little bit over two thousand years ago, while Jesus was training His soon-to-be prophetic leaders, an argument arose among them as to which of them should be considered the greatest. Their thinking was not yet fully in alignment with the ways of the Kingdom of God. If it were, they would have instead modeled the way the greatest Leader carried Himself in their midst.

But since they failed to perceive it by observation, Jesus diffused the argument by saying the following: "The kings of the nations lord it over them; and those in authority over them are given the title, 'Benefactor.' But not so with you! On the contrary, let the greater among you become like the younger, and one who rules like one who serves… I myself am among you like one who serves."[71]

| A PLEA TO THE UNSAVED

We must be reintroduced to the Creator's original intent for leadership. This error is a direct consequence of our declaration of independence from our Source. By doing so, we lost touch with who we were and the original intent of our Creator for our lives.

But there is good news: "The Creator is committed to fulfilling His purposes for us, which He initiated when He first created us. Yet, in order for Him to accomplish what He originally purposed for us; He first has to reconnect us to Himself."[72]

If you were to die today, do you know beyond a doubt where you will go? If you are unsure that means you are still disconnected from the Creator, so here is my plea to you. Put this book down right now, and in your own audible voice: confess your sins, make a heartfelt declaration to turn from your sins by renouncing them, and ask Christ Jesus, the Son of God to give you His Life and to make you a new creation. It is the most important decision that you will ever make.

Firstly, it will reactivate in you a sense of divine destiny right here on earth. Secondly, it impacts your life beyond death. According to the World Bank Data, global life expectancy is at an average of seventy-two years,[73] which is nothing but a grain of fine sand in comparison to eternity. In that eternity to come, you will either be a ruler or in infinite torment in hell. Which one would you rather experience?

| HE HEALS THE BROKENHEARTED

Brokenness will carve within us a deep sense of desperation for the Lord. Most Christians in the western world never experience greater depths in God because they are not desperate enough. We usually turn to things and activities in an attempt to escape from this reality.

Furthermore, most of us do not like to get messy or to be talked about. However, when true desperation sets in our hearts, we will no longer care about our surroundings or personal image. We must remember that if we restrain the desperate cry of our hearts, the smear of pride will continue to keep the Lord away from us. We must instead believe that the Lord loves and binds up the brokenhearted who draw close to Him.

Brokenness is necessary along the way because we get to experience healing and comfort from the Lord Himself through it, for the benefit of others. If we take our pain to the Lord, as the apostle Paul says, the Lord with comfort us in all our troubles, so that we can comfort those in any trouble with the comfort we ourselves received from God. [74]

A CRY OF ANGUISH

In my own experience, I had just gotten the ultimate slap in the face. I was no good, doing no good, and headed nowhere good. But I was given an invitation. When my guest left, I spent that evening on the floor, wetting the carpet with hot tears, and crying aloud in anguish "Jesus I don't know what to do, please help me!" It was a messy scene.

It is possible that King David was in a similar state of distress and isolation when he cried out *"Make haste to help me, O Lord, my salvation."*[75] I did not know how to pray. Well, I still knew how to recite what is commonly known as the Lord's prayer and the Catholic Rosary from memory. But at that moment, I did not care for formulas, eloquent and elaborate prayers.

I was unaware that my cry was prophetic and in perfect alignment with God's will. It was consistent with Jesus' instructions on prayer as written in the Word of God: "When you pray. Don't babble on and on like the pagans, who think God will hear them better if they talk a lot… because your Father knows what you need before you ask Him."[76] I had tried every formula in the book, and I was through with them.

A NEW THING

I was desperate to be delivered from this hell that I was living in. For the first time in my life, I was truly at the mercy of God. If this Jesus was still intervening in people's lives, then I wanted Him to hear the deepest and unfiltered cry of my heart. I was not led to say a cute "sinner's prayer." Heck, I did not even know what salvation meant. I just knelt on the floor and cried out from the top of my lungs. As I cried, I could relive every scene from my childhood flash like faded pictures in my mind. It is as though I was being led to let go of the past.

The Lord was doing a new thing and making a way for me in the wilderness.[77] The weeping went on till late into the night and I fell asleep drenched in warm tears, mucus, and cold saliva. Desperation is truly a messy affair. I woke up the next morning inexplicably joyful and at peace.[78] It was as though a dark cloud had dissipated from above me. The peace and love that I was experiencing was indescribable yet physically tangible in my inmost being. I felt alive.

Truly, God heals the brokenhearted and binds up their wounds. We need to have an experiential knowledge of this truth. The call of a prophetic leader involves "getting God's tasks and projects done through His people and moving them forward in the Lord's purpose"[79]. This is inherent to the call; therefore, true prophetic leaders must become vessels of healing and restoration because they are called to deal with broken vessels.

Since we cannot give what we ourselves do not have, we must receive healing and restoration from the Father before we can truly minister it to others. While God can use brokenness to reshape us into what He intends us to be, it is ultimately meant to serve and benefit others.

| GET REAL WITH GOD!

This is a good place to take another moment to ask the Lord to search your heart. Are you experiencing brokenness in a certain area of your life? Have you made it plainly known to God or are you content wearing a plastic smile around people while you are indeed suffering within? What if your area(s) of brokenness is (are) the areas the Lord intends to redeem to turn you into a vessel of glory? Are you willing to surrender to your heart's cry for healing and restoration?

Remember the words of R. Loren Sandford: "In the days to come a new generation of leadership will emerge, one trained in hiddenness and purified in the crucible of brokenness. Wholeness and humility will be their hallmark." The Lord is determined to preserve His Seed in this generation.

With the magnitude of end-time harvest that is upon us, the Lord is looking to release a company of prophetic people who stand humbly before Him. They will be entrusted with the treasures of heaven because they will neither usurp the glory of God nor lord it over His people. [80]

Walking in Repentance

Repentance is a beautiful thing. Yet at the mention of repentance most people, including Christians, grimace in discomfort. Beloved, it should not be so. The devil knows the devastating impact that this fundamental biblical truth can exert on his kingdom. That is why he works tirelessly to keep us away from truly experiencing its benefits.

Yes, Satan has darkened the minds of the saints concerning this truth for far too long. Unfortunately for him the Word of God states that knowledge will increase in the end times. This also means that hidden and stolen truths that were meant to make the Church an unstoppable force on earth will also be restored. We have entered a season of reckoning, and repentance is one of those biblical truths that must be restored in the body of Christ.

The similarities between the revelation that prophet Bobby Conner received from the Lord concerning the *Dread Champions* and prophetic leaders are plentiful. In his book, he argues that one of the key requirements to receive divine commission in the days ahead is purity, because purity produces power and boldness. In fact, he makes a rather bold statement in proclaiming that the church's timidity in this hour is a testimony to our carnality! How sobering when we consider that the righteous are supposed to be bold as a lion!

It is critical for these end-time champions to hear the whisper of the Holy Spirit if they want to walk in boldness. As we recall, our assignment rests upon our ability to hear what God says, and then to bring it forth by either living it out or speaking it out. Yet, the truth is: we can only be as bold as the strength of the last revelation we had.

Jesus did say that He only does what He sees the Father do, and only says what He hears the Father say. That was the source of His boldness! That cannot be done if we do not walk in holiness. For us, repentance is the bedrock upon which holiness is established.

| THE HIDDEN TRUTH OF REPENTANCE

Expanding on the hidden power in repentance could be another book all by itself. Here is what is important to note for our current discussion. There are two Hebrew words most often translated "repent" in the English language. When put together, these two Hebrew words capture the hidden meaning of this ancient truth.

The first one is a Hebrew word made up of the two Hebrew letters *"Sheen Beyt,"* which means to *"return or to turn about"* in English. These letters, when studied using the Hebraic pictographic language, speak of:

- Sheen: teeth (destruction)
- Beyt: tent (dwelling place)

The second one is a Hebrew word made up of the four Hebrew letters "*Noon Yod Chet Mem*," which can mean "*to groan, or to regret.*" Here is the symbolism of these four letters when studied in the Hebraic pictographic language:

- Noon: preservation of seed (or life)
- Yod: hand (mighty work)
- Chet: fence (separation)
- Mem: massive water (or chaos)

According to ancient Hebrew, repentance really encompasses a two-level process. Firstly, it is initiated by the destruction of a dwelling place *(the carnal state)* with the intention to never come back therein *(complete change of heart)*. Then, the change of heart ensures the preservation of life *(seed of God)* through a mighty work of God, by separating it *(the seed)* unto a place of refuge *(consecration/holiness)*, from the outer chaos. Wow!

This is the working understanding that the prophets of old, Jesus, and His disciples had when they heard: "repent!" Not mere superficial and perpetual mental decisions that have no ability to yield the power of God!

There can be no holiness (consecration) without repentance. We must stop kidding ourselves. Holiness is truly effective in yielding the power of God in the believer's life when the seed of God (Christ in us) takes root in the field of our hearts without competing with the desires of the flesh.

We may be able to fool each other but we are not fooling the world. They know when they are in the presence of a believer living in compromise, or one who lives a consecrated life. And if the world cannot tell, then the demons ruling over their lives can. They can be better fruit inspectors than most Christians, and it is only by bearing the Fruit of the Spirit (character) that they will see us as the trees of righteousness, the planting of the Lord that the prophet Isaiah foretold.[81]

As Bobby Conner affirmed: "In these days the Spirit of Truth will open our eyes to behold deeper truths hidden in Scripture, and our ears will be attuned to hear the slightest whisper of the Holy Spirit."[82] Repentance is one of the deepest treasures of Scriptures to recover in the body of Christ if we must walk in holiness. It is the separating principle that sets a hedge of protection around His Seed in us.

As you recall, prophetic leadership has everything to do with preserving the Seed through which God's purposes are accomplished on the earth. This starts with personal repentance.

| REPENTANCE IS NOT OPTIONAL

God can use just about anybody and anything to reveal His glory on the earth. But He longs for the church to become the living standard of justice and righteousness on the earth. If we want to faithfully fulfill prophetic destiny, then cultivating a sincere heart of repentance is imperative.

As the Apostle John said, we can never say that we are without sin, that would be deceiving ourselves.[83] At the same time, we cannot continue to live in sin and pretend to be His representatives. Even then, for those who believe, the Holy Spirit is more than capable of making us dwell in a realm that cannot allow sin to find expression in our lives.

We saw in the previous chapter how the Lord uses brokenness to produce humility in us. Without humility we cannot receive His grace, and without grace we cannot approach Him. Once we come to Him, He desires to give us divine empowerment, and we receive divine empowerment through God's anointing.

For the anointing to remain pure and produce the boldness and power for which it is given, we must be pure. Purity is evidence of the rulership of Christ (God's Seed) in us. That seed can only take root and grow upon the foundation of repentance.

His command is for us to be holy in all our conduct [set apart from the world by our godly character and moral courage], just as our Father in heaven is holy.[84] This is not a suggestion; it is a command. Somehow along the way, the church has forgotten that Jesus is the Lord of Hosts, the Captain of the Host of the LORD.

Those that are repentant and under the covenant of grace are no longer under the power of sin. In fact, for a repentant heart under true grace, it is harder to commit a sin than it is to be holy! God is not a man that He shall tell a lie. Nor is He in the business of setting His children up for failure. If He commands us to be holy as He is, then we must believe that it is possible because He has given us His Spirit to help us in our weakness.[85]

For the prophetic leader, or the Dread Champion if you will: "Holiness is not optional; instead, it is essential to the Lord's abiding and powerful presence in our lives (Hebrews 12:14). The Lord is looking for a people He can promote, show Himself strong, and fully support everything they put their hand to do. (2 Chronicles 16:9)"[86]. Because holiness is not optional for us, repentance is also a requirement on the path of true spiritual progress.

| LIFESTYLE OF REPENTANCE

Repentance is not just about sin as many believe. Moreover, to only associate repentance with sin speaks to the glaring need for spiritual maturity in the Church. For our purposes, repentance can be defined as the heart's sensitivity to recognizing that our own ways are crooked, and therefore passionately seeking to walk in God's ways. That includes sin and other areas of our lives as well.

When understood this way, it becomes possible to have a repentant lifestyle that does not produce legalism. Not that repentance from sin is legalism, God forbid.

We must understand this because the nature of the work that God has called us to requires living daily by faith and not by sight. During His confrontation with the enemy in the desert, Jesus stated that we were not designed to find our sustenance in food, but in every word that proceeds out of the mouth of God. Notice how the verb *(to proceed)* is conjugated in the present tense.

To those who desire to be led and used prophetically by the Lord effectively, the above statement may suggest prioritizing to hear daily from the Lord. This will improve our ability to live accurately by His standard, because the faith necessary to follow Him will come by our ability to hear. Yet, our hearing ability and accuracy are sharpened the more we subject ourselves to the double-edged sword that is the word of God.

Jesus exemplified a repentant lifestyle, yet no one can ever accuse Him of sinning. So, there must be a higher purpose to repentance other than mere sinful deeds. Faithful to His word, He walked this way daily. We know this because He only did what He saw the Father do and spoke only what He heard the Father say.

His words and actions were faithful expressions of the Father's desires in real time. He was wholeheartedly consecrated, not in terms of sin alone, but more importantly in terms of purpose. Jesus submitted Himself (mind, soul, and strength) to the will of the Father. In turn, the Father revealed His daily purposes to Jesus during their time of intimate fellowship.

| A REPENTANT HEART WALKS IN REVELATION

Today's Christians dread sin as if it is more powerful than the God who dwells inside of them. Part of the reason is that they still don't know who they are in Christ, and they have not yet surrendered to the call of God. How much bolder would we be to approach the throne of grace if we came to debrief *(receive intelligence on a classified matter)* the King concerning His business?

Instead, most Christians spend more time pleading their cases before the King regarding sin. We are no longer slaves to it, are we? The quicker we accept this reality in our hearts and not just make it a Sunday slogan, the faster we will travel the path of spiritual progress. As we will see later, surrendering to divine purpose has the power to discipline us.

We will need to be in tune with His voice and seek His ways every step of the way if we desire to see the fulfilment of God's promises.

That is one of the reasons God did not disclose the fullness of the promise to Abraham right away. He had to forsake his ways (repentance) and become intimate with the ways of God along the way.

If we walk with God the way Jesus did, revelation (a sovereign and prophetic disclosure of a secret information) would be a natural overflow in our lives. The problem is men only desire to act based on facts. This is especially true in western culture. We always want to *figure it all out, to earn our way, to quantify everything* and we try to carry that Greco-Roman mindset into the things of God. Let me quickly help you: this will never work, and it never has.

God operates through revelation, and *revelation is not figured out: it is revealed* in the corridors of an intimate walk with the Father.

Revelation transfigures the hearts of men and has the power to conform us to the image of Christ, whereas information only affects the mind. Therefore, it is common to see many believers "change their minds" over and over only to go around the same mountain for years. They never seem to appropriate the reality and power of repentance in their lives because they are fixated on performing for God instead of desiring God.

| LOVE BASED OBEDIENCE

But we can only desire His ways to the extent of our love for Him. To that effect, Jesus said in John 14:15 *"If you love me, you will do my commandments."* The assumption here is that we would do what He commands us to do out of love, not to earn a grade on our performance.

There is a relational component that enables us to desire His commandments in such a way: sonship with God the Father through the Holy Spirit. In other words, as sons *(yes ladies are sons too, just as gentlemen are also the Bride)*, we willingly obey the King as a natural love response.

Prophetic leadership requires a repentant lifestyle. I am not talking about walking around in guilt, shame, or condemnation. If you are, receive freedom now in the name of Jesus! I am not even talking about being so sin conscious that we isolate ourselves from the grace and love of God. We never want to end up in that ditch. Instead, it is about having a heart firmly established in the love of God, and a mind surrendered to the Lordship of Jesus Christ.

Wilderness and Trials

The apostle James said in his epistle: "Come close to God, and He will come close to you."[87] We just established that experiencing brokenness is necessary during the training of a prophetic leader. This is because brokenness humbles us, which in turn attracts the grace of God. The grace of God then enables us to turn (repent) and to come to God. We also saw that when we give in to Him, He is excited to meet us exactly where we are.

Now, if God is Spirit as the apostle John says[88], then it is only natural that He introduces Himself to us through means other than the natural. If most of our initial encounters with God take place in the physical realm (which is what we are most familiar with), at some point along the journey we will be introduced to the spiritual realm where He dwells.

To lead prophetically – or to lead a prophetic life, one must be acquainted with the Spirit of God and His invisible ways. The reason is simple: what He is calling us to is impossible to accomplish without us learning to lean on His Spirit.

However, to lean on the Lord's Spirit, one must be delivered from the power of circumstances and from self-ambition. To that effect, Jeremiah Johnson says: "The wilderness is the training ground for every true prophet of God. It destroys fleshly ambition. It wrecks the need to be seen. It teaches humility in ways that none of us can teach ourselves, destroying every fleshly confidence in self until nothing remains but a purified hunger for the Lord Himself."[89]

| THE TEST OF PROMOTION

Promotion in the spiritual realm often comes with some form of resistance. This is simply because as we mature from one stage to the next, our character must also be conformed with the greater authority with which we are entrusted.

For instance, when you get a job promotion it may take some time for you to adapt to the new position or environment. This may explain why some organizations often account for a *grace period* otherwise called *training*. This is for you to be firmly established in your new role, and to build confidence as you become more comfortable with the weight and demands of your newly given authority.

The job training period shares some similarities with the wilderness. God allocates a measure of grace in seasons of wilderness as we get our footing set on firm foundation. On the other hand, if we fail to display the requisite character necessary to effectively steward weightier levels of glory, we will be revisiting the same tests until we succeed. Likewise, if the newly promoted individual does not live up to their new responsibilities or does not use their new influence effectively, they may be demoted to their former role until further notice. It is a little bit of a stretch, but hopefully you get the point.

A SIGN OF ASCENSION

Take Jesus for instance. As soon as He was baptized in the Jordan river, the gospels record that the Father in heaven spoke and publicly appointed Him as His Beloved Son. By doing so, Jesus was effectively promoted in the spiritual realm, and He was now about to begin His ministry. But notice how immediately He was taken *up* -which speaks of an ascent- into the wilderness by the Holy Spirit to be tempted by Satan.

Jesus had just been affirmed as the Heir of God the Father publicly, and as the saying goes: with great power comes great responsibility. Satan was enraged. For about two thousand years he had been working tirelessly to prevent this day from happening.

He also knew that the wilderness was the Father's way to confirm Jesus in His newly given authority. So, he attempted to trick Jesus into surrendering his authority like he did with Adam. Make no mistake, your ascension into a new realm of spiritual authority will almost always be met with some form of trial.

Satan tempted Jesus to prove His newly given authority by using His own will, strength, and power, versus resting in what His Father had already established. Jesus knew that the way of success in the spirit realm is submission to the Father's will and rest in His Word. As a result, He did not bite. He knew that His success in fulfilling His destiny was predicated on His death to personal ambition and reliance on the Spirit of God.

At His weakest moment, He was tempted to prove His deity, His authority over angels, as well as His rulership over the entire world's systems. Yet, He remained content in the Father's promise and refused to act out of character. As a result, He was clothed with power as He came out of the wilderness.

Can you now see that the wilderness was Jesus' test and evidence of His promotion by the Father? If you desire promotion with God, you will be tested on the grounds of wilderness sojourn.

| LESSONS IN THE WILDERNESS

Because this book is intended to bring an impartation to the life of the reader, it would be wrong to omit my own experience in the wilderness, and some of the lessons it taught me. Some lessons are best taught through stories, and spiritual things are often better caught than taught. With that, let us journey together through some of the Lord's dealings in my life.

1– Cure from the religious spirit

The wilderness will strip you from the pollution of the religious spirit, and/or introduce you to the ways of the Spirit. After crying out to God in anguish for an entire night, I woke up the next day to an inexplicable sense of peace and joy. It is as though I had acquired a heightened consciousness of God throughout the day.

I experienced salvation without fanfare and without people bowing their heads in a Sunday church service. I didn't even know what being born again meant at the time. More importantly, I was free from the traditions of men. In the wilderness, no manmade formula or tradition will sustain you. Indeed, if "… anyone is in Christ, the new creation has come: the old has gone, the new is here!"[90]

2– Aligns the messenger with the message

The wilderness will help you understand that the events taking place in your life can be indicators of the kind of grace(s) you will eventually communicate or impart to your generation. In my case I was unchurched but I was hungry. All I knew was that I could sense that old things had passed away and that I was given a clean slate.

This was a prophetic picture of what the coming harvest will look like. It will be a mixture of people who did not grow up in church, of some who grew up in church without knowing God's true nature, and of others who have gone astray from God for a season. Their common denominator is that they will all be hungry for true spiritual substance in Christ.

> Jesus picked twelve men who had no training in religious studies and made them His disciples within three years. They had just been born again by believing in Jesus, yet they were a bunch of unlearned misfits – according to religious standards – who were hungry to see the Kingdom of God.
>
> As a prophetic person the wilderness will engrave the Lord's message in every fabric of your life. Even more so, if you are called to be a prophet, you are not just called to be a messenger of the Lord, your life is meant to become the message.

3– Kills personal ambition

The wilderness is meant to kill your personal ambition. To do so, your ability to resist the devil will be tested. Satan and his demons only make an appeal to the things we secretly crave for.

Satan is a shrewd economist, and because he knows his time is short, he is wise enough to study our weaknesses to capitalize on them. If you remember, he waited for Jesus to reach the point of utter starvation to offer Him bread. It is possible that Jesus, still fully human, may have thought about food to Himself at that moment, and Satan saw an excellent opportunity by crafting his attack according to the present need.

> As James says: "… each person is being tempted whenever he is being dragged off and enticed by the bait of his own desire."[91] In the wilderness your desire to make things happen in your own strength will be stripped. Like Jesus, you will need to learn from Moses by speaking to the Rock instead of striking it. Failure to learn this lesson early may be costly to your destiny.

4– Produces child-like faith

The wilderness will lead you to the gates of the Kingdom of God, which you will enter by walking in child-like faith. Typically, this will be done through the work of brokenness as discussed earlier. You must learn to live by faith by developing trust in the manifestations of the Spirit of God within your heart and not according to your will or circumstances.

> God will ensure that you experience both the joy and peace of the Kingdom of God while at the same time giving little to no source of happiness in your external circumstances for a season. This is so that you learn to build your reliance more on spiritual truths over material realities.
>
> In my experience, my circumstances did not change overnight. I had the same problems, but they no longer preoccupied me as much. I became childlike at heart, full of joy, and all I wanted was to know God. As Jesus pointed out: "Yes! I tell you, whoever does not receive the Kingdom of God like a child will not enter it!"[92]

5– Leads to the Kingdom

The wilderness will establish you in the reality of the Kingdom of God. It will cause you to overlook your earthly problems and set your affections on the unseen realm. In my experience, I went from agonizing about my circumstances to really embracing my alien status on earth.

> Meanwhile, my sense of belonging was being fulfilled. I felt right at home in an invisible world. I began to flip through pages of the Bible and stumbled on a passage that said that my citizenship was in heaven.[93] I did not immediately know what it meant, but it sure sounded good to me. All along I "… was looking forward to the

city with permanent foundations, of which the architect and builder is God"[94], and it embraced me with open arms. At last, I had found a home.

In the wilderness your appetite for the realities of the Kingdom of God will grow. On the contrary, your appetites for worldly fulfillment will decrease.

| IMMEDIATE TESTING

In the wilderness God will immediately put your early victories in the walk of faith to the test. Earlier, we saw how Jesus was *immediately* driven to the wilderness after baptism. The Spirit of God Himself drove Him there for the explicit purpose of being tested by Satan.

God may allow these trials so that He may intervene in our lives supernaturally. Remember, the nature of the call to prophetic leadership requires that we rely on His Spirit for advancement. How can He train us to rely on His Spirit unless He sometimes allows us to be in situations that require His supernatural intervention?

| DOORS INEXPLICABLY BEGIN TO OPEN

Here is how this worked out in my own life. Before I could really understand what was happening to me after salvation, I began to experience the reality of this invisible Kingdom. A few months prior to salvation, I had applied for a master's degree in information security at the university. Because of my unique circumstances, the only way possible for me to attend school and remain in the country legally was to work as a Graduate Assistant in my field of study.

I had reached out to the Dean multiple times for a position in vain. I can still hear his words echoing in my mind: "I only have three full-time positions and they are all taken. Try next year." The only problem is, I did not have the luxury of waiting another year, something had to happen now.

However, a few weeks after salvation and confessing the word of God daily, I received an email from the same Dean asking me if I was still interested in a Graduate Assistantship position. He explained that he was somehow able to split his three full-time positions into six part-time positions. He further stated that I needed to meet with him on the next business day if I was interested because he had a long list of applicants.

A few hours later, I received another email from the university asking if I was interested in working as a computer help desk student worker. Before I could respond to that email, I received a call from a Samsung representative begging me to be their brand ambassador at the local Best Buy. I told them that I was flattered but my work permit had expired and that I had to wait for my enrollment at the university to even be allowed to renew my Driver's License. They said not to worry about it and to come for a formal interview. I hung up the phone pinching myself.

By the end of the day, I was hired by Samsung, and by the university's helpdesk. I ended up turning down the job at Samsung because I was afraid to break the law, despite the hallucinating offer. Now, the most crucial of all was the graduate assistantship because it would guarantee that I remain in the country legally.

FIRST SUPERNATURAL ENCOUNTER

The following business day, I woke up and thanked the Lord for what was happening. I said a prayer, took a shower, grabbed my wallet, phone, and house keys off the top of my study table. Interestingly, I did not see my public transportation money next to the aforementioned items, and I took off. I joyfully made my way to the bus stop still in complete awe. Just when I thought that life was finally smiling at me, my new-found faith was *immediately* put to the test.

I noticed the bus arriving at the horizon and reached into my pockets for the bus fare. They were empty. My heart sunk; it is as if the world came crashing down on me: not again! The math was simple: If I ran back to my apartment, I would miss the bus. If I missed the bus, then I would miss my interview. If I missed the interview the Dean would fill that position with someone else and that would have been my return ticket to my birth country. I stood there spiritless and playing this scenario in my mind.

Suddenly, I felt a bubbling forth rising from within my belly and I inexplicably opened my mouth and said emphatically: "Jesus, if You want me to remain in this country then I'm going to swipe my student identification card as a credit card to pay for the bus fare and it is going to work!"

Now, I very well knew that my card was not working at the time because I had tried to use it in vain on the university's campus shuttle a few days prior. Also, this was not the campus shuttle, it was the city bus.

My declaration sounded almost as absurd as telling a physical mountain to move and expecting it to happen. There was no evidence for me to believe that this was possible, but as Jesus said: "… everything is possible for someone who has trust!"[95]

This was the decisive moment. The bus stopped. I stepped in, swiped my expired ID card through the bus fare terminal in faith and the light went green. I could not believe it especially because as an IT Specialist by trade, I understood 1's and 0's, and I knew this was simply impossible. I was on time for my interview and got hired on the spot.

TRUE ENCOUNTERS BIRTH HUNGER

That day the Lord revealed Himself to me in a tangible way and I embarked on a passionate quest to know Him beyond the scriptures. He had crossed the invisible realm and manipulated binary sequences to show me favor. It is as though He was yelling: "You may not see Me but for a moment you touched Me. If you seek Me, I will be tangibly involved in your daily life!"

I was not going to settle for knowing about Him through others any longer. I had to know Him personally and experientially. Beloved, this is eternal life, that we may know Him, the only true God, and Jesus Christ whom He has sent.[96] Supernatural experiences of divine favor began to multiply in my life, the kinds that will cause your jaw to drop, and the length of which would take me several pages to write down.

At last, I was genuinely loved in this newly found home. Whenever folks would detect my accent and ask where I was from, I would boldly say "heaven" because I was experiencing the reality of the scriptures daily.

> "I will go before you and will level the mountains; I will break down gates of bronze and cut through bars of iron. I will give you hidden treasures, riches stored in secret places, so that you may know that I am the Lord, the God of Israel who summons you by name."[97]

| TESTS OF FAITH ARE NECESSARY

Beloved, tests of faith are necessary for the life of every believer. Only faith that has been tested can be trusted. If trials are necessary for every believer, they are inevitable for those with a prophetic destiny. Abraham's faith was tested when God asked him to offer up his only son Isaac as a burnt offering.[98]

Before we ignorantly rebuke the enemy at every little trial that we face, it is important to remember that it is the Spirit of the Lord Himself who drove Jesus to the wilderness to be tempted by the Adversary.[99]

The enemy may be involved in our trials or seasons of wilderness sojourns, but it is only by divine permission. He is a tool that God, in His sovereign will, can temporarily allow to disrupt our lives for His own eternal purposes. It is important to note that Satan cannot act beyond God's authority. Therefore, we should not empower him by giving him more attention than the Lord, as He prepares us for the task ahead.

TRIALS ARE GATEWAYS TO THE SUPERNATURAL

You have probably received a prophetic word of destiny. If you haven't yet, may the Holy Spirit reveal the Father's will for your life. For those who have, do you remember the feeling of empowerment that followed and how your faith was reenergized? Let us remember Joseph. He had a dream of his destiny, and woke up a changed man, sharing it with his brothers. I believe he did it out of excitement, and not to provoke his brothers to jealousy.[100]

But right after seeing his future greatness, he found himself at the bottom of a pit. If that wasn't enough, he was sold into slavery. The moment he began to have favor with his master, he was wrongly tossed in prison for doing the right thing. I can only imagine how he felt throughout this process. Yet, Joseph never complained and instead he continued to serve others while in prison. I wonder how different the story would've been if in the dream Joseph was also shown the ensuing trials that he was going to face.

Trials are entryways to the Kingdom of God. Many Christians desire to experience the miraculous and the supernatural. However, most of us do not want to be placed in situations that require the miraculous hand of God to see us through.

On the other hand, although miracles and encounters can often be defining moments on our journey with God, they are not meant to be the end goal. Most trials are an invitation to seek deeper intimacy with the Lord of the Kingdom. Genuine authority in the Kingdom of God is obtained on the bedrock of intimacy with the Lord, which is essential for effective prophetic leadership.

Intimacy: The Source of Prophetic Leadership

| THE LORD IS A JEALOUS GOD

Outcomes can be unpredictable and well-meaning people can sometimes be unreliable, but "Jesus Christ is the same yesterday, today, and forever."[101] If we are called to live and lead prophetically, we will inevitably have to learn not to put our trust in man, or in promised outcomes.

It is commonly accepted across the body of Christ that we should not place our trust in man. After all, most people have heard or read a version of the following statement at a church or in the marketplace: "The heart is deceitful above all things… and cursed is the person who trusts in humans".[102] Yet it is not as obvious for many to realize that we should not trust in God's promises more than we trust in Him either.

Many have come short of intimacy with the Lord because they desired the promises more than they desired closeness with the promise-giver Himself. Jesus spoke of a category of people who have embraced the promises made concerning the gifts of the Holy Spirit and who successfully walk in it. Yet, in the same breath He also points out that He will reject some of them because He never "knew" them.

The verb *"to know"* used here is the Greek work *"ginosko,"* which originates from a Jewish idiom for intimacy between a man and a woman. The Lord causes the sun to shine and the rain to fall on both the believer and the atheist. Therefore, enjoying the promises made by God is not necessarily proof that our trust is in Him.

| THE PROMISE OR THE PROMISE-GIVER

The Lord will ensure that we learn this truth by sometimes giving us seemingly strange instructions that will reveal the degree to which we trust in Him over man or promises.

For instance, God promised a son to Abraham at the age of seventy-five years old. After twenty-five years of walking with God as a friend, the long overdue promise came to pass in the birth of Isaac. But God did not desire to become second fiddle to Isaac in Abraham's heart. Therefore, He commanded him to offer his only son, as a sacrifice.

Can you imagine what went through Abraham's mind? If the man had desired a son more than he desired friendship with God, he would have doubted Him in this matter. Who would blame him? But as the story unfolds you can see how Abraham trusted in the God of the promise more than the outcome of his faith in the promise.

The Lord makes us promises as He draws us to Him, and He also will require us to put these promises on the altar of sacrifice to see if He is truly the center of our affections.

This is how this unpopular truth worked out in my own life, early on in my walk with the Lord. As soon as I genuinely gave up pursuing women, the Lord gave me a detailed description of my future bride at the condition that I never again approach a woman because He was going to bring her to me. When she came in my life, though she was a gift from the Lord[103], He always made sure that no one would cause me to drift apart from Him. We had a special bond, and He wanted to preserve it at all costs, and so did I.

I can confidently say there is no breakthrough that I have experienced in my life by the independent will of a man, none. I am extremely grateful to the people that have blessed me in different seasons of my life, and I always go above and beyond to genuinely express my gratitude towards those who have helped us over the years. I am also aware that it is God who inspires those men to bless me, whether they realize or not.

Lastly, I also know that God will remove from my life anyone that attempts to take His place in my heart. If you are called to be one of His Dread Champions, this will be common in your life, so get used to it.

A STRANGE INSTRUCTION

I too was given a seemingly strange instruction concerning the promise. It only took a few months before I realized that God would not even allow my wife to share His space. He wanted me to create a special space just for her, but only if she came second to Him alone.

Before becoming one with a spouse, we belong to Him, and because of that, He has every right to be jealous of us, being His prized possession.[104] As I contemplated proposing to her, the Lord instructed me to first give her an ultimatum. It went like this:

> "The next time you meet, tell her that you love her dearly and that you want to make her a queen. Then tell her that you will never love her more than you love Me and that you will never put her before Me. Lastly, tell her that if she is not willing to have the same attitude towards Me, then she must leave your property immediately and never return. If she is on board, I will bless your union and make you inseparable. If she isn't, then cut her loose immediately. No one else will seat at the throne of your heart but Me."

I obeyed and she stood by my side through every trial. Because she knows the Lord's place in my heart, it also allows her to strengthen her own trust in Him, knowing that He must come first in Her life for us to fulfill our common mission.

| GOOD CAN KEEP US FROM GOD

The enemy can use any good thing that the Lord has given us as an obstacle to the fulfillment of divine destiny. This is not to make you fearful, but to make you watchful. If we learn to put things and people in their proper place, we will be able to see how the Lord has uniquely designed them to assist us on our way to fulfilling prophetic destiny.

Peter, out of zeal and love for Jesus opposed the idea of his Master's death. That resulted in a severe rebuke from Jesus because Peter was thinking from a human perspective, not God's perspective.[105] The Lord's response shows that the Father and His will have priority over our lives.

Prophetic leaders must understand that once they commit to trust in the Lord, He will be opposed to anything and anyone that threatens His supremacy in our hearts. By doing so, the fulfillment of His promises will become a byproduct of our relationship with Him instead of the goal.

What are some of the things and people that have usurped the place of the Lord as number one in your heart? Would you sincerely allow the Father to prove your heart by putting the promises He has made to you on the altar of sacrifice? If you received the fulfilment of a promise, are you putting more care in its maintenance than you are seeking the Lord Himself?

Take a moment to ponder these questions and ask the Holy Spirit to adjust your heart posture where you feel conviction. Do not let the blessing become the reason you become estranged from the Blesser. Father, let us have ears to hear, eyes to see, and hearts to recognize the place that You must have in our hearts.

| PURSUING INTIMACY

Intimacy with the Lord is a non-negotiable requirement for those that are called to prophetic leadership. We hear this word tossed around a lot lately but what exactly is intimacy? It is an uninterrupted longing for common union with the Father Himself. It manifests within us a real desire to embody the things in which He delights in. It is also a state of holy reverence that draws us to the secret place, where our authority is validated.

Most Christians have simply become too comfortable with the Lord, even to the point of familiarity. That form of presumptuous familiarity is responsible for the widespread contempt towards the Lord masquerading as disobedience. It is a fallacy for anyone to claim intimacy with the Lord without consecration.

At its root, consecration means "to set apart." How much of our lives have we set apart unto the Lord? Or do we commit spiritual adultery daily and hope that our Sunday lip service is something attractive to the Lord?

The mark of effective prophetic leadership is spiritual authority. The key to true spiritual authority is found in deep intimacy. "The church is crippled by a lack of intimacy.," said Jeremiah Johnson. The one thing that should captivate the heart of a prophetic leader is not a platform, an open door, a breakthrough, success, or a new connection: It is the presence of the Lord.[106]

If we genuinely believe that our fulfillment is found in Him, then why do we exert so much energy drinking from the wrong wells? How often do we spend time at His feet in prayer and hearing His word just to know Him? Instead, many of us are doing these activities with the purpose of finding the next clue to our business' success, preparing the next sermon, looking for Bible verses to satisfy our own desires.

How good can that be? Even Satan used scriptures in his attempt to derail Jesus[107], so how does that make us any different? Do we really believe that eternal life is to *know* God and Him Whom He sent? [108] Here goes that word "*ginosko*" again. Unless we develop an intimate walk with the Lord, we cannot effectively claim to exert the level of authority that His Life is meant to give us on this side of heaven.

If we are reduced to seeking the hand of God and not interested in touching His heart, then we are still walking as immature children. While a child usually waits for the father's death to receive their full inheritance, a bride's immediate inheritance is the groom himself and everything that he has.

| LET THE FRUIT MATURE

On a certain morning as I was fasting and praying, I inquired of the Father's heart concerning what the church should be turning its attention to. Then, I heard Him say that He desires *maturing fruit*. Let us consider John 15:16 "You did not choose me, I chose you; and I have commissioned you to go and bear (produce) fruit, fruit that will last, so that whatever you ask from the Father in my name He may give you".

Our Lord Jesus was a Jew, talking to other Jews. Here the English word "*name*" is the Hebrew word "*shem,*" which means "*character, authority, honor.*" Naturally, fruits come from trees, and they need to ripen before they are eaten, otherwise they are not pleasant to the taste. Figuratively speaking, fruit can symbolize anything that results from an act or a deed; hence we often say "*the fruit of my labor*" to describe what we have produced by our work.

Elsewhere, we are taught that "the fruit of the Spirit is love, joy, peace, patience, kindness, goodness, faithfulness, humility, self-control."[109] We can clearly see that the attributes of the fruit produced in us are linked to character. This fruit is the only kind that can last because it is produced by Holy Spirit, who Himself is everlasting. When our character reflects the fruit of the Spirit, then we honor Jesus, and access to greater spiritual authority is imparted unto us.

| CHARACTER MATTERS

After hearing the Lord say that He desires maturing fruit, I then asked Him to elaborate a bit on that, and He gave me the following illustration. A teenager may aspire to get married someday and they may even imagine what the ideal spouse should look, talk, and act like.

However, as the teenager matures into adulthood, those criteria usually end up changing. As a result, the person that they end up espousing may look, talk, and act very differently than what their teenage-self once desired. They cannot therefore not afford to relate to their partner according to their old (immature) standard of the right spouse.

Likewise, the Father desires the fruit of the Spirit to mature in us so that we can contemplate Jesus (our Groom) with the right lenses. As we grow in character through the maturing of the fruit of the Spirit within us, we are propelled into higher realms of understanding, love, and intimacy with Jesus. Let us ask the Father to fertilize the soil of our hearts so the fruit of the Spirit may ripen (mature/grow) within us, so that we may experientially become one with Jesus.

We do not pray to have the fruit. It was already planted in the soil of our hearts as a seed. An apple seed contains an apple tree, it just needs to be grown. Likewise, we pray for the maturing of the seed that He has already placed in us. This is consistent with 2 Peter 1:3 "God's divine power has given us everything we need for life and godliness. Through our *knowledge* of the One who called us to His own glory and goodness."

One of the best ways to know someone is to become intimate with them. Probably the most intimate way of knowing someone is to become their spouse. The prophetic leader must mature and learn to walk in the dimension of the bride of Christ.

| THE BRIDE OF CHRIST

There is a creeping lie in the body of Christ stating that as soon as you become a professing Christian, then you are automatically the "Bride of Christ." Unfortunately, it is simply not so. The entire church (all believers) is not the bride (at least not right now), but the bridal company is made up of some people who are part of the church.

The Bible is full of types and shadows that point us to deeper truths. In the twenty-fourth chapter of the book of Genesis, Abraham instructs Eliezer his servant to go to his country and retrieve a bride for his son Isaac, specifically from his kindred. Before we go any further, it is crucial to lay out the types and shadows represented here:

- Abraham in Hebrew means *"Father of a multitude."* He is also known as the founder of the Jewish nation and the father of our faith. We can see here that Abraham is a shadow of our Father in heaven, the Ancient of Days.

- Isaac was Abraham's only son[110] according to God's covenant. Isaac was the seed of the promise. He represented a type of the Only begotten Son of God, Jesus, who is the Son of the Promise. He is famously known for being led to the slaughter by his father without resistance, which was a prophetic allegory to Jesus being led like a lamb to the slaughter.

- Eliezer was Abraham's servant whose name means "*To whom God is help*"[111]. In John 14:16, Jesus gives us the Holy Spirit as the Comforter. The word Comforter is the Greek word "*parakletos,*" which in the widest sense means "helper." Eliezer's name is only mentioned once, and the rest of the time he takes on a self-effaced persona who is always pointing to his master Isaac. This is remarkably similar to how Holy Spirit operates: always pointing us to Jesus.

- Abraham did not just want a woman from his country (citizenship), she had to be picked out of his kindred (family members). Now, we know that those of us who are born again make up the church. Furthermore, according to Paul we are no longer outsiders, but we share citizenship with the saints, and we belong to God's household.

Intimacy is not required for someone's salvation. But it is a prerequisite for those who desire to fulfill their prophetic destiny. Prophetically speaking, we have Abraham (Father) instructing his servant (Holy Spirit) to go to his family (the church) and retrieve *a* bride (singular) for his son Isaac (Jesus). Have you begun to see it?

If you read the story carefully you will notice that Eliezer, faithful to the charge that was given to him, gave himself an additional requirement for the bride.

As we saw earlier, it was common for young women to draw water at the wells. He expected most young women in that town to be hospitable and to give him a drink upon request. So, he determined that the bride would stand out from the crowd by *going beyond what was asked of her, without being required to do so*.[112] She was not required to give water to the camels to be part of Abraham's family, but that was the prerequisite to become Isaac's bride!

Eliezer brought gifts for the bride and her entire family, and on the way back to the promised land, Rebecca became so acquainted with and captivated by Isaac that she ran to him while they were still far away. Without the shadow of a doubt, as they journeyed several days back to the promised land, Eliezer taught her and groomed her ahead of the encounter with Isaac.

| THE BRIDE PREPARES HERSELF

Eliezer's role in the story above is a shadow of the Holy Spirit's operation in our lives: He comes with gifts to the church. But only those who truly desire to *know* Jesus (*intimately*) will be willing to be led by the Holy Spirit to set their affections on Christ.

Even though Rebecca was the chosen bride and enjoyed every privilege that came with that distinction, *she made herself ready* before ever meeting Isaac physically. "Let us rejoice and be glad! Let us give him the glory! For the time has come for the wedding of the Lamb, and *his Bride has prepared herself…*"[113]

Some of you might still be doubting but make no mistake: not every professing "Christian" is the bride of Christ. We might all be saved but we are not all the same in God's Kingdom. Consider the following.

After a man proposes to a woman, he still observes her from a distance. He is observing to see if her character is made of the right stuff, and vice versa. If during the engagement period you find out that your future spouse is sleeping around with other people, you more than likely will not make them your bride. So, if as imperfect people we have certain standards for whom we espouse, how much more do we think Jesus would?

| ENGAGED, AND UNVEILED

If our faces are already unveiled, it is for the purpose of being changed into His image from one level of glory to the next.[114] In principle we are still engaged to Jesus because the marriage of the Lamb takes place at a future time according to scriptures.[115] However, because the Lord tore the veil between heaven and earth, He has therefore made it possible for us to live from His eternal dwelling place and walk as His bride right now.

Beyond giftings and anointings, the Holy Spirit is here to captivate our hearts and brand us with bride-like character. In return, we must be willing to yield to the leadership of the Holy Spirit. If not, we are deceived to think that we can be careless in our relationship with Him and claim to be the Lord's bride.

It is true that Christians who are not at this moment part of the bridal company are still saved and can enjoy God's blessings. However, there is another dimension that is beyond salvation and sonship, for those desiring to go deeper into intimacy with the Lord. As His bride, we truly come to learn how to be one with Him.[116]

The dimension of the bride is not a position or title, rather a disposition of the heart we should develop if we ought to walk in our full inheritance and fulfill our specific role(s) as His partners in the final and greatest harvest that He has prepared for our generation.[117]

The good news is that there is no trick to walking in this dimension: bear fruit that is born out of intimacy. We are told the fruit of the Spirit is made up of specific character traits, and you will notice that *feelings and intellectual knowledge* do not make the list.

People with genuine prophetic destiny are generally consumed with fulfilling the calling of God. But that can only happen if they live a life surrendered to knowing the Lord intimately and espouse His purposes in their hearts and through their lives.

| HELPMATE

The apostle Paul likened the relationship between Christ and the church to that of a husband and wife for a good reason. The first wife according to scriptures was Eve. She was designed to be a suitable helper to Adam. A helper is someone who comes along to another to provide support or assistance in accomplishing a certain goal.

I am not saying here that God needs man's help for anything, He is God Almighty, self-sufficient, and omnipotent. What I am saying however, is that God has historically chosen to partner with the agency of mankind to accomplish His will on earth, as it is written: "The heavens are the heavens of the LORD, but the earth has He given to the children of men."[118] If we are the bride of Christ, then we must also desire to partner with Him to fulfill His purposes on the earth.

| MOVING ON TO PROPHETIC PURPOSE

Many desire to walk intimately with the Lord and probably lead a consecrated life. Many others, over the course of their journey with the Lord may have even considered the call of God upon their lives. Yet, if the call to live and lead a prophetic life is present, it may be difficult at times to know whether what we perceive to be our divine purpose is indeed from the Lord.

If God desires to work through us to preserve His Seed and advance His kingdom on the earth, then it is important that we have a way of identifying true prophetic purpose. As a reminder: prophetic leaders are those who can hear what God says and live it out with the fundamental purpose of helping others access their own place of divine inheritance.

The following section will help us identify some key elements of true prophetic purpose, and how to cultivate your prophetic leadership potential.

PART THREE

CULTIVATING PROPHETIC LEADERSHIP

Prophetic Purpose

| TRANSCENDENCE

As prophetic leaders, we must have the firm conviction that our existence is not an end to itself. God has a purpose much bigger than what we often allow ourselves to see. If He has called us, then there must be something He is calling us to. As His bride, we are called to be His "helper" in accomplishing His will on earth. This involves the entire world, and then tiny little us.

Jesus gave several discourses on effective prayer. One of them is commonly known as "the Lord's prayer." It is widely understood that Jesus was instructing His disciples on the elements of a model prayer. Given our context, we can see that this model prayer also reveals orders of magnitude, or levels of priority, for those who desire to lead prophetically.

Prayer is the spiritual technology that we use to communicate with the Lord. Prayer is also the means through which we, as the King's magistrates, enforce His decrees on earth. If we are supposed to hear God's word and to live it out in a way that helps others find their own place of divine inheritance in Him, then it is important to know the Lord's priorities.

"Our Father in heaven, hallowed by Your name, Your kingdom come, Your will be done on earth as it is in heaven. Give us this day our daily bread..."[119] Read that again, but slower this time. Did you notice how the Lord mentions a personal need (daily bread) only after catering to the Father's will concerning His agenda?

| SEEK FIRST THE KINGDOM

The sequence of statements in this prayer is not a coincidence. It communicates the level of importance of each aspect of prayer, in decreasing order. The highest order of priority here is the kind of relationship that gives us ground to approach the Lord *(identity in Christ)*. The second is our heart disposition as we come before the King *(reverence)*. The third is the coming *(or advancement of)* His Kingdom. The fourth is His will, which must be done on earth *(man's domain)* the same way it is administered in heaven *(God's domain)*.

Many of us do not enter our prophetic destinies because we are still immature and self-centered in our prayers. Most of our prayers sound like this "My needs, my kids, my family, I, help me, me, my..." God does not call us for the mere sake of paying our bills and improving our living standards. Having a decent job alone can accomplish that much, so that must not be it.

The world can easily offer the things that most Christians fast and pray for. I say this with tears. Meanwhile, the truth is that the Lord will meet our needs while we prioritize the things that matter most to Him.

The Father desires that our affections centers on Him and His purposes. He can take care of us, and our needs better than we ever could. Would we not trust and enjoy a spouse that seeks our interest, whilst knowing without a doubt that we seek theirs? That is the way the Kingdom operates: Jesus entrusts and enjoys us the more when we seek His interests, while being confident that He always has our best interest in mind.

In Jesus' effort to educate His disciples on this matter, He stated: "seek first the Kingdom of God and its righteousness, and all these things will be added to you." Once again, Jesus prioritizes the Kingdom and the righteousness of God over personal needs. But He assures us to provide for those needs as we pursue Him.

You see, God is only required to provide for our current (daily) needs if we are actively engaged in the pursuit of His Kingdom and living according to His will for us here on earth. There are no guarantees of divine provision or protection for us outside of God's will, according to the allocations He made for us in His Kingdom.

| A TECHNOLOGICAL ANALOGY

Just like a product cannot serve its creative purpose outside of its manufacturer's original intent, man cannot truly discover the true purpose for his existence apart from God the Creator. I once owned a Computer and IT Services business, and I have personally serviced all kinds of Apple devices as an IT Specialist.

In creating an iPhone (product), Apple (creator) provides a wide range of software updates (care) for its product for as long as it has the potential to operate in conformity with Apple's original intent (purpose) for both the end-user and the company. The software updates are akin to current provision, supplying the iPhone with what it needs for its effective daily operation, and Apple guarantees its supply.

Once Apple determines that the iPhone can no longer optimally serve the end-user in a way that reflects the company's current vision and objectives, Apple will discontinue its support. Yet, that iPhone will always be an authentic Apple product, even though retired.

Just like Apple is no longer obligated to provide *automatic* support for an outdated iPhone, God is under no obligation to provide for us daily if we pay no attention to His Kingdom's agenda and His will. And just like the obsolete iPhone remains an Apple product, we will yet remain His children. But truly, just like Apple guarantees support for an iPhone that has the potential to serve its original intent, Jesus assures daily provision for us when we serve His will according to the purposes of the Kingdom.

If you still find yourself fasting, praying, seeking, and toiling for the things of this world, instead of them being provided to you as you engage with prophetic destiny, there is a good chance you have not yet found your purpose in the Kingdom of God.

| PROPHETIC INTERCESSION

If the Lord has a purpose for the earth, then we as His bride, are the entity qualified to bring forth His plan. The other characteristic of the bride is that she is a friend. Aside from the Lord, I consider my wife to be my closest friend because I spend most of my time on earth with her. She knows all my whereabouts, my strengths, and weaknesses, and she knows my plans because I discuss them with her. "Surely the Sovereign Lord does nothing without revealing His plan to His servants the prophets."[120]

Recall that at his core, a prophet is someone whose very life becomes the fulfilment of a divine mandate. The word "prophet" in the context of this specific verse carries the added notion of a familiar worshipper chosen and beloved of God, on account of piety and approved fidelity, to accomplish His objectives.[121]

The kind of worshipper described here is firstly an ambassador called and sent by God, with whom God is familiar: this is only possible by spending intimate time with Him. Secondly, they do not engage in spiritual adultery. Thirdly, they remain faithful to His word. Lastly, they surrender their lives to the fulfilment of His purposes. It is therefore safe to say that a true prophet and prophetic people (believers in general) can also operate in the dimension of the Bride both relationally and functionally.

Abraham was an intimate friend of God and because of that, the Lord referred to Him as a prophet. Abraham never spent a minute preaching in a temple, but he was an intercessor. We saw it the first time God calls him a prophet. The Lord made sure to mention that his prophetic task was to intercede for the women in Abimelech's camp. We also see how the Lord consulted with Abraham before destroying Sodom and Gomorrah. I desire that level of influence with God, do you?

If yes, then perhaps it is time we effectively seek first the Kingdom of God and its righteousness like Abraham did. We have the mind of Christ[122], let us rise above self-seeking and make the business of the Kingdom of God our priority.

STOPPING AN ACT OF TERRORISM

This is one example of how this has worked out in my own life. On September 17th, 2016, my wife and I were invited to dinner at her parents' house. We were expected to arrive at 4 PM. I was praying in the Spirit earlier that afternoon because I felt we would come home late, so I wanted to have time alone with the Lord beforehand.

About an hour into prayer, I began to feel a sense of anger and discontent rising from within. I knew it was not from my own heart because I had nothing to be angry about. So, I started interceding by praying in tongues, pressing through to get rid of this growingly revolting feeling, but it remained. At this point, I heard my sweet wife knocking on the door to inform me that it was nearly 3:30 PM. I wanted to get out and get ready, but the Spirit of the Lord rested upon me so strongly that I was compelled to ignore her.

As I tarried in the secret place and continued to move in the Spirit of intercession, suddenly, I began praying in plain English against terrorism in my city (St. Cloud, MN), completely unaware. It is as though the Holy Spirit had bypassed my mind and hijacked my mouth without my knowledge.

When I caught myself praying against terrorism, it took me off guard. I thought to myself: "why would I pray that?" Then I knew that the Lord had just given me the interpretation of tongues[123], and the spiritual intelligence necessary to bring forth His purpose in this matter: safety from an imminent act of terrorism my city.

At this point, the level of urgency in my prayer rose and I was able to strategically pray against terrorism at the Crossroads Mall. Also, the Holy Spirit revealed that the enemy chose that location because it held the largest concentration of people on a Saturday in the town of St. Cloud.

Around 5 PM I finally felt the release to go, yet I quietly remained in the spirit of prayer the entire time during the trip. A little while after dinner, as we were fellowshipping at the table, I pulled up my phone and read that there had just been an act of terrorism at the same mall in my city. Many were injured but fortunately no life was lost, and the suspect was taken out by an off-duty police officer who happened to be shopping in the same store as the terrorist. The mall was shut down the entire evening, as law enforcement took over.

I am in no way saying that I, Ulrich, was the one who prevented the worst from happening. But I am convinced that the Lord did something as I stood on my knees for hours in my room, crying out to God on behalf of the lives of others. What if I had chosen to ignore this urge to pray by prioritizing my desire to get to dinner on time? Boy, my wife was upset (understandably so), but after seeing the news and hearing my side of the story she was thankful to God for my obedience.

True prophetic leaders are intercessors. Although not all intercessors are prophets, prophetic intercession is a sure sign that one carries such a calling. Prophetic leaders carry the burden of the Lord for the people and nations of the earth. They also lift the burdens of the people to the Lord. They stand in the gap and cry out to God on behalf of others for prophetic revelation and guidance which sometimes avert crises and plagues in cities, regions, or even nations.

They willingly embrace the fact that their lives are not their own, and that the agenda of Kingdom of God supersedes theirs. Unless you regularly give yourself to intercession (praying on behalf of the purposes of the Kingdom of God and of others), you cannot claim to lead a life or to be led according to prophetic purpose.

| JUSTICE AND RIGHTEOUSNESS

One of the sure signs that prophetic purpose empowers us is that we have a zeal for righteousness and justice. Righteousness and justice are the foundation of the Lord's throne.[124] Psalms 9:4-5 declares: "When my enemies turn back, they stumble and perish before You. For You upheld my cause as just, sitting on the throne as the righteous judge."

Notice: King David used the word *"when"* instead of *"if."* That means he expected his enemies to stumble and to perish. But he also reveals that his success was certain because the Lord validated his mission as a just cause - one that was noble and righteous before the Lord.

The Lord is the righteous Judge, and He created us to rule on the earth according to His standard of righteousness. If we walk in the fear of the Lord and give ourselves to deep intimacy with Him, we will inevitably begin to channel His hatred for evil.[125] Therefore, it would be an oxymoron for us to have a divine purpose which does not bring justice to people or oppose evil in any fashion.

When I first heard a father in the faith describe the "dread champions" during a sermon in the Fall of 2018, I could not help but assimilate them to the kind of prophetic leaders that the Lord is about to unleash on the earth. They champion a noble cause, which they often believe to be in response to an evil that tees them off.

YOUR PURPOSE PRECEDES THE EXISTENCE OF EVIL

You see, most people think they suddenly woke up from their slumber to embrace a just cause because of the darkness that is upon the land. The parable of the wheat and the weeds, and the parallel illustration with Churchill and Hitler seem to suggest otherwise. In both instances, God planted the good seed with noble intentions *before* the enemy raised one in direct opposition.

The darkness that is covering the earth is proof of the preexisting purposes of the sons of Light. Your prophetic purpose preceded you because it existed in God before you were formed in your mother's womb. So, it is natural for every believer to hate evil: that is part of our spiritual DNA if we are truly born of God.

The preexistence of truth provides the basis for a lie to be formed, just as darkness is best described as the absence of light. In reality, the evil on the planet is a deliberate attempt to prevent us from manifesting the dimension(s) of Light given to us.

I prophesy that there is an army of men and women who will arise, knowing that the Lord will support a just cause. You were not just born to solve a problem; that problem exists to reveal what was buried inside of you all along.

GOD IS NOT LIMITED BY RELIGION

As mentioned in the first section of this book, the Lord can use any man who is desperate for justice and righteousness. This is true even if they are not your typical religious person, like Churchill for instance. This might surprise you, but it can be a good thing. God never asked for humanity to be religious people. In fact, He might sometimes face less resistance when using non-religious people.

The Oxford dictionary defines religion as a system of faith and worship.[126] That sounds to me like practices created by men with the purpose of hiding their lack of trust and obedience in the Creator. Obedience is a truer act of worship and a more expressive sign of trust than following rules and engaging in manufactured activities. But that is separate teaching altogether.

NOBLE MOTIVES ARE USEFUL TO GOD

God in His sovereignty can elect to work through a man simply because of a noble motive, even if they are not born again. While Joseph was in prison, God spoke to Pharoah in a dream. So here, Pharaoh heard the voice of God, though he did not know at the time who was speaking to him. But because he further listened to the custodian of the wisdom of God within his territory (Joseph), he effectively saved the life of the sons of Israel.

Jesus came from the tribe of Judah, one of the twelve sons of Israel. We might rightly say that Joseph produced the plan to prepare against famine, and therefore he deserves the credit. However, none of that would have happened if Pharaoh refused to yield to the Spirit of wisdom and understanding operating through Joseph.

Indeed, God can use a pagan ruler to preserve His Seed and further His purposes on the earth. Pharoah perhaps thought the dream was only about saving his people from starvation. That is the noble, just, and righteous thing to do for any sensible leader. Because of his heart's disposition God was able to preserve the coming of His Seed (Christ).

If God can do that much with pagans who can yield to His wisdom, how much more can He accomplish with a believer who champions a noble cause?

One of the sure characteristics of a true prophetic leader is that their assignment carries an element of justice and righteousness. However, just because someone champions a just cause does not make them a prophetic leader.

As we saw earlier, God is the one who calls prophetic leaders. They must therefore reflect some of His attributes. One of those attributes is a heart of love and compassion for humankind, which often manifests in hatred of evil.

| SENSITIVITY TO EVIL

Unlike most people, prophetic types usually have a higher sensitivity to evil. We cannot claim to have the fear of the Lord and be indifferent in the face of evil and injustice. This sensitivity is heightened even the more for those who are called as prophets, because prophets not only live their personal lives, but they also live the life of God.

What this means is that prophetic leaders are wired to hear God's voice and feel His heart. They try to impart the anguish of the burden that they carry, and as imparters their souls overflow from the fullness of their compassion.

The following story will give you an idea of how God can sometimes make us aware of this inherent sense of justice and righteousness. Since impartation is one of the goals of this book, here is an example of how the Lord revealed two of the evils that tee me off.

| AN INCIDENT AT THE LAKE

In the summer of 2014, my wife Rebecca and I were on a date at a lake in St. Louis Park, Minnesota. We sat down on a bench facing the water. Behind us were a pedestrian trail and a mobile restroom on the other side of the trail to our left. I was ranting about the injustices of life and the increasingly inconsiderate nature of humankind. I looked up to my right and saw a family walking towards us.

I also immediately noticed that one of the boys appeared to be physically impaired. Immediately, I quietly asked the Lord why such injustice: why was this boy born with a handicap and I was not? I was troubled. They slowly walked by us and stopped a few feet away to our left.

The disabled boy signaled to use the restroom across the trail. I watched him helplessly, as he carefully looked to his left and then to his right, making sure no one was skating or biking towards him. I followed along and saw that the path was clear for him to safely proceed. Right on cue, as he slowly strode across the trail, two men on bicycles literally ran him off the trail. He somehow managed to contort his body just enough to avoid getting hit.

They had more than enough time to slow down, but they did not. They did not care to look back either, but they yelled at him instead. I thought of catching up with them, but they were already beyond reach.

I was enraged: just a moment ago I was ranting about the increasingly inconsiderate nature of man, and this took place almost simultaneously. Like John the Beloved, every ounce of me wanted to call down fire from heaven to consume these knuckleheads, but I knew better. Soon thereafter, the boy finished his business, and they began to walk away.

Suddenly the anger turned into a fight-or-flight type of response. The further they went away from our bench, the more my heartbeat increased, my hands trembling, and my palms sweating. I did not know what was happening to me, but I knew I was supposed to bring justice and fight for that boy.

Whilst most people view injustice as harmful to the welfare of the people, to the prophet it is a deathblow to existence: for most, an episode; to the prophets, a catastrophe. To the prophet, even the slightest injustice assumes cosmic proportions.[127]

Prophets are people who feel fiercely; thus, their speech and acts can be outbursts of violent emotions. Prophetic people also have a higher sensitivity to evil than the rest of humanity, although the prophets tend to operate an octave higher above the pack.

So, I stood up and ran after them anyway. Once caught up with them, I told the mother I was sorry for what had just happened. She replied that the boy had autism. With a somewhat sluggish tone she said: "It is okay, this kind of stuff happens to him all the time, we are used to it." As though she had resigned to the fact and accepted it as the norm for her child.

But she did not know the manner of man she was talking to. The man in front of her was experiencing both the righteous anger of the Lord towards the injustice, and His divine compassion towards this beautiful soul. To her surprise, I rebuked her and told her "It should not be!"

While I was still talking, the boy came up to me, hugged me tightly, and lingered for a while. At that moment, the only words that I could utter were "God loves you, and I love you, my friend." I tried to formulate other things, but I did not have words. When I got home, the Lord told me that He wanted to put my own words to the test and see what I would do.

THE BLESSING OF RIGHTEOUS ANGER

He also revealed that He allowed me to witness this scene because He was stirring up my heart for justice. A phrase that prophet Bobby Conner prophesied to me the following year at a prophetic conference.

The other thing that the Lord revealed to me that night was compassion for the sick. I had always felt compassion for those who are sick and handicapped, but I never knew why. This episode revealed that He was also stirring up my heart for healing and restoration, which He eventually began to manifest in my life and ministry.

We are anointed to bring the Lord's justice and righteousness in our respective sphere of influence, including within the church. Can you think of some incidents in your own life which provoked you into righteous anger? Take the time to recall them, take notes, and ask the Lord to confirm by His word or through trusted prophetic voices, whether your life is the antithesis to that problem.

In the name of Jesus, I pray that the Lord confirms the way(s) in which you are meant to administer His justice and righteousness on the earth. Because this is so critical given the harvest that is at hand, I pray that He does so without delay. Amen.

| SERVING HUMANITY

We can never claim to love a God whom most of us have never seen, while at the same time have no love for humankind, whom we can see. This means we can determine whether someone really loves God by their attitude towards other men, since man is created at the image of God. The same is true in matters of prophetic destiny. We can never claim to have a prophetic purpose that serves the Lord if we are not able to prove that it serves humankind.

In practice, the fulfilment of destiny often occurs as we serve our gift, whatever it may be, to those in our generation. Dr. Myles Munroe was used by the Lord to train leaders from all professional backgrounds around the world. Very few men possessed the divine and practical wisdom he displayed as a leader.

He once recalled that one of the recurring questions people asked him during his leadership seminars was the following: "How can I know if my vision as a leader is inspired by God and merits the support of many people?" After much contemplation and meditation, he concluded that a purpose that does not aim to improve, enhance, and relieve humanity of things that destroy it is likely not inspired by God.

In other words, any desire to lead that only benefits you does not originate from the Lord.[128] It is that simple.

God commanded king Solomon to ask Him for anything he desired. Solomon asked for the wisdom to lead God's people in a way that would ensure their welfare. In return, God not only made him the wisest man to ever live besides Jesus, but He also ensured Solomon to have the support of his people and every material blessing he needed at his disposal during his reign.

Solomon put his people's welfare first and God took care of his needs. What about the greatest leader of all? Jesus made it His primary concern to serve humanity, instead of looking to be served. In return, the Father made sure that He would be served by the very ones that He first served. Do you see how this works?

True prophetic purpose will make us obsessed with the Lord's business, and the Lord will take care of our business while we conduct His and serve humanity. This matters because God chose humanity as His chosen soil to carry His seed and advance His purposes on the earth.

| GLORIFYING THE LORD

True prophetic purpose must aim to serve the purposes of the Kingdom of God because we receive directives from the Lord and our agenda should be for His will to be done on earth as it is in heaven. One key aspect of such a purpose is that it usually sounds unrealistic.

God uses the foolish things of the world to confound the wise, and His foolishness is wiser than human's wisdom. In other words, if you can rely on your logical mind to fulfill your purpose, then there is a great chance that it is not of the Lord.

The reason for this is simple: if we can do it with our own strength and might, then we would not need to rely on God to accomplish it. This would be contradictory to the necessity of living by faith and putting our trust in Him. Additionally, it would disprove our need to depend on the Holy Spirit. But what the Lord purposes in and through us can only be done "Not by might nor by power, but by My Spirit says the LORD Almighty."[129]

Also noteworthy is the fact that the Lord does not share His glory with any mortal.[130] The destiny that He has prepared for us is simply too complex to be conceived in our own minds. Furthermore, its burden is too heavy to be fulfilled in our own strengths. Otherwise, we would take the credit for fulfilling them instead.

If God allowed Abraham and Sarah to age beyond their strength before giving them a child, it ensured that they would never be tempted to praise themselves in the birth of Isaac. Sarah's unbelief was understandable, it simply looked logically impossible. Thus, they knew the child was born due to a supernatural act beyond their natural inability to procreate.[131] Perhaps this aided in making it a little easier for Abraham to offer Isaac as a sacrifice. Since the Lord showed Himself faithful in His promise, Abraham trusted in God's character and faithfulness.

True prophetic purpose is not logical. In fact, it offends the carnal mind because the things of the Spirit are hostile to the things of the flesh. We must learn to develop our trust in the Lord if we are to fulfill it, and that kind of trust can only come through personal dealings. Through those dealings, we will learn to glorify the Lord at every turn.

INTIMIDATING

The fact that prophetic purpose challenges our logic can sometimes make us reluctant to do what God is asking of us. Part of that hesitancy comes from the enormity of the task at hand, and the fact that we do not believe we are qualified, able, or adequate to do it.

The Lord has a reputation of baffling human wisdom by using the less likely to carry out a great destiny.[132] Gideon is a prime example of this. When called by the Lord to lead the Israelites' army, he rapidly objected: "Pardon me, my Lord … but how can I save Israel? My clan is the weakest in Manasseh, and I am the least in my family." But the Lord replied: "*Surely I will be with you*, and you will strike down all the Midianites, leaving none alive."[133]

This is probably the most important phrase that prophetic leaders long to hear from the Lord during their journey. Their lives are meant to execute the Lord's purposes; therefore, they understand that they can only be successful if *He is in it with them.*

Prophetic purpose is usually weaved into every fabric of our lives. We must understand that all the events that take place in our lives – successes, trials, failures - serve to prepare us for a future moment when destiny finally calls us to action. For those of us who are spiritual, "we know that God causes everything to work together for the good of those who love God and are called in accordance with

His purpose."[134] We must know beyond a doubt that we are called to things bigger than ourselves, if indeed we believe that it is now Christ that lives in us.

There must be an unwavering sense of divine destiny brooding within us. Like Churchill, Gideon, and many others, we may not necessarily know how things would pan out. But we can be confident if God has given us a glimpse of the future that He envisions for us.

As we journey with Him, we will come to trust that He has already made provision for it, because He is the author of the purpose for which He created us. Our role is to be proactive with the vision to secure His provision.

Cultivating Prophetic Vision

| THE NEED FOR ACTION

It is impossible to accomplish anything of significance with inaction. This is true in world and biblical history. It is most certainly true when it comes to the prophetic leadership concept. In 1910, Theodore Roosevelt explained in his Citizenship in a Republic's speech:

> "The credit belongs to the man who is actually in the arena, whose face is marred by dust and sweat and blood, who strives valiantly ... so that his place shall never be with those cold and timid souls who neither know victory nor defeat."[135]

The church often majors in finger-pointing and criticizing those fellow believers or leaders who may have fallen from grace. Meanwhile, we have minored in bringing healing through divine solutions as the agents of transformation we are meant to be.

It is important to bring correction to those in error. It is even more important for the church to respond to our calling and usher in the spiritual and cultural reformation our generation desperately needs.

Criticism is merely a reaction to the evil one. But greater influence is born on the merit of action, not reaction. We cannot be wishful and hope for God's promises to manifest on their own.

Your purpose is a state of fulfillment that the Lord set in motion when He created you. This means that your birth, which marks the beginning of your life here on earth, is the evidence of a specific purpose that the Lord intends to fulfill. Your salvation marks the starting point of its fulfilment because you need to be reconnected to the Creator for you to be introduced to that purpose.

The good news is that if we apply ourselves to the purposes of the Lord in our lives we are guaranteed to succeed. After all, He is "declaring the end from the beginning and from ancient times things not yet done, saying, 'My counsel shall stand, and I will accomplish all my purpose'".[136]

That state of fulfillment, however, is discovered from within and requires some digging. We must understand that having a sense of purpose and identity in the Lord is not enough to bring reformation in our culture. The Lord has planted seeds of destiny within our hearts—His garden—and our role is to cultivate this "land" if we want to bear the expected fruit.

The expectation of fruit is a display of faith, and the walk of faith requires wisdom. I absolutely love the book of Proverbs in the Bible. In fact, it is the first book that I read from start to finish after salvation. At that time, I was in serious need of direction and wisdom, and frankly, I still am. We are forever in need of God's wisdom if we live by faith.

Every time I study a Proverb, I realize that the answers to some of the questions that went unanswered in my life for years are written in one of those thirty-one chapters. As a result, it has become clearer to me that "… many of the great truths that should have been the domain of the church have been stolen by the world and put to less than noble use."[137] Now, let's examine some of the Proverbs to find some wisdom on how to act on the vision we have received from God.

| WE ARE FARMERS

"He who farms his land will have plenty of food, but he who follows futilities has no sense".[138] This statement carries such importance that it is revisited in the book of Proverbs a few chapters later.[139] I took the liberty to dig into this a little deeper and my findings were quite refreshing.

The verb "*farms*" aforementioned is the Hebrew word '*abad*, which means "*to cultivate.*" The word "*land*" is the Hebrew word '*adamah*, from the root word '*adam* which is also the name of the first man. Elsewhere in the book of Genesis, we learn that man's ('*adam*) first assignment was to *cultivate* the land and care for it.[140]

It is interesting that the first task that God gave man was to cultivate the land in which he was placed. Also, God placed the spirit of man in a body formed from the dust of the land. Hence, land ('adamah) was the root word from which the name of the physical man was derived. This is incredibly significant.

As mentioned earlier, names usually revealed a person's character and authority. In our context, Adam's name essentially meant "land." By naming the first man as such, God ensured that the condition of the land was forever linked to the character of man. Now it becomes clear why land is the first thing that God cursed on the account of Adam's sin.

Man's primary assignment is not to affect the world around us, but to develop the man within. From the origin of his name, cultivating the land had two applications for Adam. First his character and authority, since he is made up of the same substance as the land under his feet, and then his surroundings.

On the other hand, the second part of Proverbs 12:11 states that "he who follows futilities has no sense". In other words, our dedication to cultivating our inner man – or character – will bring us fulfillment. Whereas running after things that are unworthy of our calling takes us away from discovering and cultivating the seeds of greatness within us.

According to the Merriam-Webster online dictionary, to cultivate means "to prepare or prepare and use for the raising of crops."[141] This underlines our need to understand who we are, which if unaddressed will lead us to spiritual and material unfruitfulness.

| CULTIVATING THE "INNER MAN"

The concept of cultivating our inner man may seem too abstract, so let us view it from a practical standpoint. In agriculture, cultivating the land is a vital task. In fact, most soils are not ready to produce plants or trees unless they are first cultivated or tilled. Cultivating as a practice accomplishes two main things. Firstly, it removes weeds from the soil. Secondly, it loosens the soil to optimize the retention and penetration of water, air, and nutrients.

The need for cultivating is found in the fact that nature, over the course of time, takes a toll on the soil in the form of foreign - non-organic - junk, rain, foot traffic, etc. These contribute to compact the land over time, therefore resulting in a hardening of its surface.

Cultivating the soil brings up weed seeds - bad seeds - to the surface, therefore exposing them to nature's hazards, which causes them to die. This, in turn, ensures that the good seed will compete less for water and nutrients. As I wrote in *Cultivating Your Inner Man*, this contributes to the good seed being optimally fed and produce a healthy plant.[142] Based on this brief study on the process of cultivation, let us see how it relates to us.

Just like the course of time negatively affects the soil, the course of life has several ways to take its toll on us: work, friends, stress, daily responsibilities, hurt, family, hobbies, etc. Those things, though good for some, can clog up our lives and wear us down. Examining Proverbs 12:11 within our context reveals that God is not merely giving a piece of advice to farmers. He is also addressing the condition of man.

More precisely, it addresses the examination of the man within, our inner man. He urges us to cultivate our character and reveal its buried treasures. Furthermore, He promises that anyone who does so will find fulfillment.

In contrast, those who lead their lives after worthless things or relationships display their ignorance of self. If they took the time to discover the seeds of greatness within, they would be invested in creating an environment favorable for their divine destiny to flourish.

Many of us in the church have received a prophetic word of destiny. We commonly refer to it as the call of God. To you who may not have an idea of what that calling is, I pray that the Holy Spirit will reveal it to you as you ask Him in faith. Whether you know what the calling on your life is or not, there are dreams that God desires you to accomplish.

This is where underachievers and achievers are differentiated: "Underachievers usually spend their lives dreaming about the day their big break will come... True achievers build their lives with strategy..."[143]. Leadership starts with self-discovery: you must be willing to discover yourself if you intend to activate your prophetic destiny.

| AN UNSUNG REVELATORY TOOL

Most Christians view professional careers or trades strictly as secular activity. Of course, a prophetic word of destiny from the Lord is a very sacred thing. Yet, God can use even the things that we consider secular in nature to help us discover some of the seeds that He planted within us. The truth is that it is a mistake to separate our professional backgrounds and skills from the divine.

For the believer, work or trades should not be considered secular. If God cares about us enough to count the hairs on our heads[144] – He probably has an easier time counting mine than yours – then He probably cares about our professions or secular occupations.

Although we are the ones doing the work, we are supposed to be filled with and led by His Spirit.

That means God can be involved in the fabric of our professional lives as well. Better yet, He wants to reveal aspects of our spiritual callings through our educational choices, past jobs, trade skills, and childhood passions.

| THE MASTER CARPENTER

In the Gospel according to Mark, Jesus was known in His hometown as a carpenter. It is in part because of it that His own folks had a tough time believing He was the Son of God. He grew up learning everything about the trade and we know that He did everything with the spirit of excellence. Also, as the first male child, Jesus was supposed to take over the family's business according to customs. But did you know that it was no accident that God the Father chose that profession for His Son?

After researching on the word *carpenter* in Greek, my findings were stunning. In Greek, it is the word *tekton*, which means *artificer*. Now, an artificer is a person who is skillful or clever in devising things. Furthermore, the word artificer originates from the root word *artifice*, which is a clever or cunning device especially as used *to trick or deceive others*. Pay careful attention to what I am about to explain.

As a carpenter, Jesus was likely an artificer of wood. In the natural world, wood is an object that lends itself well to human manipulation for creative purposes. For instance, a carpenter can creatively turn a useless piece of wood into a chair. But wood is also the object of choice for superstition and magic.

Repeatedly throughout scripture, we see the Lord rebuke the people of Israel for worshipping wooden idols. As Jeremiah 10:8 says, "a wooden idol is a worthless doctrine."[145] Prophetically speaking, wood stands for the works of the flesh or worthless human doctrine that opposes the word and the work of God. Do you begin to see where this is going?

God the Father could have chosen Jesus to be a tax collector or a physician, but instead, His profession was that of a carpenter. This was not a simple coincidence. As an artificer of wood, Jesus was a skillful worker.

In a prophetic sense, Jesus made an artifice of human doctrines. Isn't it fitting that He ended up hanging on a *wooden* cross? While Jesus was hanging on the cross, Satan thought he had won because the cross was the ultimate symbol of death. What he did not know however, is that Jesus used the wooden cross to devise the greatest trickery in history.

The apostle Paul attests of this fact in Colossians 2:13-15 where he says "He forgave us all our sins, having canceled the charge of our legal indebtedness, which stood against us and condemned us; He has taken it away, nailing it to the cross. And having disarmed the powers and authorities, *He made a public spectacle of them*, triumphing over them by the cross."

As a carpenter Jesus worked with wood and nails. Yet, even in that trade, His spiritual calling was revealed as the one who came to destroy the works of the flesh, worthless human doctrines, and even death itself.

I used this illustration to invite you to take another look at your childhood passions, current profession, or trade skills you may have learned over the years. You might be amazed at how much the Lord can reveal to you concerning your prophetic destiny through these "secular" things.

As children of God, nothing in our lives happen by accident including our work. "For we are God's handiwork, created in Christ Jesus to do good works, which God prepared *in advance* for us to do."[146]

THE SEEDS FROM YOUR BACKGROUND

The moment we become a child of God we can see His workmanship in every aspect of our lives. Here is how this worked out in my own life. Years ago, during a mundane conversation, my biological father shared something quite revelatory with me. He told me how, at two-years-old, I dismantled his expensive brand-new stereo. He said I would get up in the morning and be immersed in taking it apart.

At the time he told me this story, I was repairing computers and mobile devices for a living. All along I had no idea it was something that I started doing at the age of two! It further reminded me of a prophetic word that I had received back in 2015. It was about being a dismantler, and how I loved to take things apart to find a problem for the purpose of restoring them. It further said that the Lord was going to use that ability in my ministry. Then it hit me: that is how my prophetic anointing usually flows in my ministry!

Furthermore, I have a background in Information Security both at the undergraduate and graduate levels. A lot of what we do involves preventing and finding security breaches. The goal being to preserve or restore the integrity, confidentiality, and availability of digital information. I have a deep passion for truth and integrity, duh! But I had never made the connection between my natural talents, secular background, and spiritual calling until that faithful conversation with my biological father!

Just to confirm, earlier this year, I asked my mother to share a bit about my childhood. She said, "as a little boy, as early as three years old, you were righteously strict towards yourself, always told the truth, and mercifully kind towards others. You also hated evil with a passion, and always longed to serve in the house of God." How we make it too complicated sometimes!

Does that make you curious to ask your parents to share some of your childhood hobbies or tendencies? Are you now willing to examine your professional skills or work activity through a spiritual lens? You might be pleasantly surprised to discover that God can use your natural talents and abilities as a map to help you find your prophetic destiny.

| ENGAGING THE PROPHETIC VISION

It is quite common to see people lift their head toward the heavens when they are about to pray. Though it is perfectly acceptable, the reason most of us do that is because somewhere deep in our subconscious mind we believe the answer to our prayer exists outside of us.

The truth is that the treasure is not found outside of us. Instead, it is within us because the Kingdom of heaven is within us. So instead of looking up towards the sky, we may want to look inwardly to the

Kingdom. If the treasure is within us, then it needs to be discovered to be useful.

A seed buried in the land will bear no fruit unless it is cultivated. The seed you carry was planted in the soil of your heart. We are awakened to its existence through the prophetic ministry. When we receive a prophetic word, it is usually confirmation or identification of what is already within you. But unless you engage with the prophetic word, it will bear no fruit. This truth can be seen in the parable of the talents.[147]

Just like the Lord sovereignly distributed different amounts of talents to the three servants, He has also entrusted us with different talents and gifts. We can see from the story that the two servants who took the initiative with their talents were able to multiply them. However, the one servant who hid his talent out of fear and indifference lost favor with his master. Not only did he lose favor with his master, but he was also stripped of the only talent that he had. In contrast, the ones who invested their talents gained favor and were entrusted with greater.

The moment we engage with the prophetic word we receive, our lives become a prophecy in fulfillment. If there is anything that we can glean from the parable of the talents, it is that God will see that what He has spoken over our lives will happen if we are diligent. As James Goll puts it, "When you choose to follow the dream that the Lord places in your heart, you are choosing life."[148]

It is crucial that we nurture and engage with the prophetic vision if we are called to express the life of God in our generation. If we do this, we will inevitably produce fruit because the seed of God when watered and nurtured will certainly produce fruit as we continue to choose His will.[149]

THE FRUITS OF FAITHFUL CULTIVATION

1– Royalty

The process of cultivating your prophetic vision will produce three essential fruits that a prophetic leader must bear. Firstly, it validates your royal status. "It is the glory of God to conceal a matter; to search out a matter is the glory of kings."[150]

Our royal identity is founded in our Kingdom citizenship through faith in Jesus Christ. But we access the greater measures of authority that were already imparted to us as we grow in character. This cannot happen unless the soil of our hearts is tilled, and the things that can choke the seeds of God's calling are removed from our lives.

For instance, Abraham would not have been introduced to the royal priesthood unless Lot was removed from his midst. Soon after he separated from Lot, he received the blessing from Melchizedek, *king* of Salem and *priest* of the Most High God. Though Abraham had accepted the call of God on his life, God did not share certain details of His plans until Lot had left from his midst. It is good to note that Abraham did not fight Lot despite his exalted status: true royalty knows its place.

Shortly after salvation, as I read Abraham's story, I started to realize that I had to put an end to certain relationships. An intense desire to move to a solitary place away from my current roommates began to grow within me. I was living a consecrated life and I wanted to grow deeper in the things of God.

I wanted to be where my Lord wouldn't need to compete with anyone else for my time, affection, and my attention. Yet I was still halfway through my current rental lease. As I thought on the situation, one day during my devotional, I ran into 1 Corinthians 15:53 "Do not be fooled: bad company ruins good character." I still remember the feeling while meditating on that verse.

It was like a sharp arrow shot straight at my heart. I had to face the facts: my environment was not favorable to a life of consecration. Late-night partying, drinking, and smoking could no longer be my daily reality if I were to take the next step towards prophetic destiny. I felt the pull towards something greater in God. Although I did not know what to expect, I knew I had to leave. But how do you walk out in the middle of a rental agreement without causing problems?

For weeks I resisted the Lord on this, perhaps a couple of months. But every day I was reminded that this environment was incompatible with my new life trajectory. So, one morning after much prayer, I surrendered and resolved to pack up and leave.

My prayer was: "Lord, I do this because I want to draw near You. This might cause grief to my roommate and will potentially have severe legal ramifications. But I refuse to miss the mark because of the fear of man. So please make it right." "Fearing human beings is a snare; but he who trusts in the Lord will be raised high [above danger]."[151] On a Saturday morning, I moved out of the apartment without a word, and I cut off every kind of contact with my former roommate.

Two weeks after moving out and living in a solitary place, I had an angelic encounter that revealed the prophetic destiny upon my life. Not only that, but the angel gave me the Abrahamic blessing. On top of that, the angel revealed my wife's identity.

Two years later, I ran into my former roommate in the streets at 3 AM in the morning. I was in the middle of a solitary six-hour prayer walk interceding for my university campus, while he was returning from the bars. He then informed me that the matter went to court and the judge ruled in our favor. The judge not only gave us the opportunity to sue the property owner, but he banned an eviction from ever appearing on our rental history. You cannot make this stuff up! I am not sure what my roommate thought of it, but I knew what had happened: The Father upheld my motive to seek Him as pure, and He caused things to work for my good.

This was yet another evidence in my own life of the Lord's faithfulness to those who seek Him with diligence. It further provided me with the encouragement that I needed to fully consecrate myself unto the Lord.

The Lord's royalty is not meant to be limited by the systems of men, but to rule over them because we are under the authority of the courts of heaven, which is a higher court. If we are motivated by His business, He will override the systems of men to exercise His authority in our favor.

If the kings of the earth are known to obtain favors from men, then we should be assured that we will have the favor of the King of all kings when we purpose to seek first the hidden things of the

Kingdom. By doing so we will discover, protect, and nurture seeds of His majesty within us.

2– Discipline

Beloved, discipline should not be regarded as burdensome. Contrary to widespread belief, true freedom lies within the establishment of boundaries. It is the absence of boundaries that leads to bondage. The apostle Paul said it best: "You say, for me, everything is permitted? Maybe, but not everything is helpful. For me, everything is permitted. Maybe, but as far as I'm concerned, I am not going to let anything gain control over me."[152]

The call to consecration requires discipline, and our sense of discipline is determined by the choices we make. Christians widely associate consecration with sin, and rightly so. But as we saw earlier in the case of repentance, limiting consecration to sin is a sign of spiritual immaturity. Beyond separation from sin, effective consecration encompasses a separation unto something higher than us.

Some of us will never be able to overcome that sinful issue unless we are captivated by a greater purpose. Sure, our greatest purpose is to be conformed to the image of Christ. But are we going to walk around with wooden crosses on our backs and march towards Jerusalem to conform to His image? Of course not. So, what does that look like in a practical sense?

This is where prophetic purpose comes in because it is the missing piece to true spiritual discipline and consecration. Simply avoiding sin is religion, and many of us are good at being religious, yet having little to no impact in our families, schools, and workplaces. However, being consecrated unto something creates a stronger magnetic field that has the power to draw us away from the lower law of sin into the higher law of prophetic purpose.

Discipline is a byproduct of our consecration unto prophetic purpose. Therefore, it does not look the same for everyone. It will take different forms according to the unique calling of the Lord for our lives.

The will of God concerning our lives is ultimately what dictates the kind of discipline He subjects us to. For instance, after dedicating myself to the call of God on my life, I had a dramatic prophetic encounter in which Father strongly told me to never ever touch cannabis. It was so vivid that thinking of it, my heart still trembles in awe of the thundering voice and authority with which He spoke to me on that matter.

I literally came out of that encounter shaking and terrified, but the message was crystal clear. For that reason, no man can ever convince me to touch it again. People around me may have sympathetic views on cannabis, and I am not here to argue with them. But like Joshua said to the Israelites who served other gods in Joshua 24:15, "as for me and my house we will serve the Lord" and cannabis is unequivocally out of question in my household. It is as simple as that.

It is good to point out that we may exhibit the same discipline as our brothers and sisters on the surface, but our underlying motives are what separates us. Hence it is important to avoid comparisons with others, because doing so can undermine your own purpose.

A professional basketball player for example, may not use cannabis. But he may be doing so for other reasons than mine. His main motivation for staying clear of drugs might be to maintain peak athletic performance, while mine are completely different.

On the other hand, the calling on my life does not require that I spend countless hours practicing jump shots, though I love playing basketball. But because of his unique sphere of influence, a professional player might be required to practice jump shots eight hours per day while I am not. He is doing so to master a skill, while I am just playing to break a good sweat.

Likewise, my assignment might require that I pray seven hours a day, but assuming the basketball player above is a believer in Christ, he may not need to keep the same prayer regimen to represent Christ in his field.

The Lord will discipline those He loves. He will also impart the grace for discipline according to His divine purposes for us, and "our goal must be to not just know Him, but to obey Him."[153] Once you have dedicated yourself to act on the vision God has given you, you must exercise discipline.

However, "we do not discipline ourselves to earn points with God. That is performance-based acceptance." Instead, discipline that "brings character formation to make you a vessel that can carry the glory of the Lord"[154] comes by revelation, not religious performances.

3– Boldness and faith

Boldness and faith have a nickname: it is called risk. This is the third fruit of cultivating the inner man. When we actively partner with the Lord to nurture and water the seeds that He planted in us, He will inevitably cause us to grow in revelation. This is crucial because our degree of boldness and our level of faith are linked to our level of revelation.[155]

Leaders are also known as risk-takers, and prophetic leaders are not an exception. We are called to live by faith, and there are no such things as being stagnant in the Kingdom of God. We are either constantly growing from one level of faith to another, or we are backsliding. In the words of Smith Wigglesworth:

> "Remember beloved, don't forget that every day must be a day of advancement. If you have not made any advancement since yesterday, in a measure you are a backslider. There is only one way for you between Calvary and the glory, and it is forward. It is every day forward. It is no day back. It is advancement with God. It is cooperation with Him in the Spirit."[156]

That is quite insightful. It means backsliding takes place long before any visible signs of regression are observed. In your journey to fulfil prophetic purpose, it is important to know whether we are making forward progress or whether we have stalled. Faith is designed to increase the more we exercise it. We cannot rely on the measure of faith we initially received at the point of salvation to face the challenges of tomorrow.

We need a new infusion of faith, as the opposition we face increases the further we intend to proceed forward with the Lord. That is why the apostle Paul exhorts us to build our most holy faith by praying in the Spirit. We must continually build our faith to advance, for we are designed to fulfill prophetic destiny by faith.

The more you take risks in obedience, the higher the stakes will grow, and it will require greater faith to make the following jump. As you develop trust in the Lord by seeing His hand at work in your life, you will come to know without a doubt that you are partnering with the Lord and that your life has become a prophecy in fulfillment.

Each time you will be presented with a daunting task, the circumstances will likely be increasingly intimidating. However, the principle will remain the same: what has the Lord revealed to you concerning the matter, and are you sure of it?

Cultivating our inner man will lead us to live a life of surrender to God's purposes. Knowing that nothing in your life is an accident helps to overcome fear when facing the inevitable challenges that leading a prophetic life will present.

The path to destiny is a perilous one and calls for the kind of courage and resilience that will ensure survival and success. True prophetic leaders have an overwhelming sense of urgency to the calling of God, and it draws them to action. They recognize that their lives have been designed to accomplish God's purposes on the earth. They will rely on prayer as their secret weapon to a breakthrough when things are humanly impossible.[157]

To walk in boldness, a lifestyle of intimacy with God is first practiced during your season of incubation when no one is watching. To trust in the Lord during adversity you will have to rely on His proven faithfulness in your life. David was able to take on Goliath publicly because He had experienced the faithfulness of God privately. He remembered God's faithfulness when he defeated the lion and the bear, and that gave him the boldness to slay the giant.[158]

Added to intimacy is the dedication to acquiring the skills that you need for your assignment while getting rid of what is unnecessary. Even though some of those things may be good, they may not be expedient to your purpose. Remember that Eve was not attracted to the evil side of the fruit, but to the good side. Though it was good, it wasn't the will of God for her. Whatever is not the will of God for us, is what Proverbs 12:11 identifies as futilities.

| FROM BELIEF TO TRUST

Cultivating prophetic vision will move us from the realm of belief into the realm of trust. Trust is a much deeper experience in God than mere belief. Scriptures teach us that even demons believe and tremble.[159] So, if all you do is believing and fearing God, then you are no different than a demon. How sobering! In several instances throughout the gospels, demons verbally expressed their belief that Jesus was the Son of God. Yet, we know without a doubt that they do not trust in Him as their Lord and Savior.

I believe that you, the reader, are a good person. But for me to trust you with my children in my absence, you have to establish trust with me. You will only reach that level of trust with me as your character is revealed through relationship. I may believe good things about you without entrusting you with something dear to me. Likewise, it is possible to believe in God without trusting Him with your life.

Cultivating prophetic vision, especially as we begin to act upon it, leads to experiencing the character of God on a personal level concerning His promise over our lives. After Joshua and his generation died, the children of Israel fell into apostasy immediately.

This new generation did not know the Lord, nor the works that He had done with their predecessors. Furthermore, it never occurred to them to dig into their spiritual heritage to find out what worked for the previous generation. Thus, they believed God to be God, but they did not have their own experiential revelation of His character.

Consequently, they lived in constant defeat even in their promised land. We must give ourselves to cultivate the seeds of prophetic destiny in our inner man, so we may eat the fruit of the land that is promised to us. If we fail to do it, the gravitational pull to engage in futilities will be too strong for us to fulfill the calling.

Practical Guidelines

| YOUR IDENTITY AND SCRIPTURES

Perhaps the greatest crime in the history of mankind is identity theft. From a cybersecurity standpoint, it is the fastest growing crime in the western world. It is vital that we discover our identity and that we be secure in our identity.

Just like ill-intended individuals would steal our identity online, the enemy has been successful at stripping us from our identity. He has even found ways to substitute it with good and honorable things like ministry.

Unfortunately, many of us confuse our identity with our activity. But the process of discovering – or rediscovering – our identity is fundamentally determined by our experiential knowledge of scriptures. More specifically, we are who the word of God says that we are in His eyes, not ours.

If we are truly saved, the indwelling presence of the Holy Spirit will awaken us to the reality that we are God's children. Our journeys are all different, however, and it could be more difficult for some to really be secure in their identity as sons or daughters of God. How do we then become secure in our identity in Christ? Once again, discovering it starts with becoming students of the word of God. This is fundamental.

If we rely on another person's revelation, we will not have the backbone necessary to resist temptation. If Jesus - who is the Word Himself - relied heavily on scriptures to resist the enemy throughout His entire life, then we are not exempt. Lack of familiarity with the word can have devastating repercussions on our lives, even more so if we are called to lead. To help others get to their place of divine inheritance, the word of God must be our foundation.

| STUDY AND MEDITATE ON THE WORD!

Studying the word of God is a more involving activity than merely reading. Knowing someone by their name doesn't imply you know them. Similarly, quoting scriptures doesn't necessarily imply we know their Author. As we study scriptures let us learn to slow down, ask questions to the Holy Spirit, take notes, and seriously ponder on the things that we read.

The goal shouldn't be to memorize or understand every single verse: that can only lead to frustration. The goal is to encounter Christ as you meditate on them. The more you encounter Him through scriptures, the more you will become like Him.

The word of God is inexhaustible, so be patient with yourself. But also, be sensitive to the Spirit as He leads your study time. Developing the habit of spending uninterrupted time alone to quietly study and meditate on the word is perhaps the most important investment we can make.

It is through consistent meditation of scriptures that we grow in discernment. I suggest it be done daily. Recall that we are in a spatial war between good and evil, and the word of God sets us on the right course. It is our GPS, our spiritual and moral reference on any matter. If you can find a believer who struggles with their identity in Christ, then you have a great probability of finding someone with insufficient communion with the word of God.

| HAVE A TEACHABLE SPIRIT

Equally important, "All scripture is God-breathed and is valuable for teaching the truth, convicting of sin, correcting faults and training in right living; thus, anyone who belongs to God may be fully equipped for every good work."[160] I have come to find out that the scriptures that initially offended and challenged me the most ended up being the ones that accomplished the most profound transformations in my life. Consider them all.

Especially spend extra time on the ones that your mind initially rejects due to offense or unbelief. Ask the Lord to shine the light of His countenance on your understanding, that you may be inwardly transformed.

Let us labor to love Bible verses that offend us or contradict our personal or cultural beliefs. They are often the ones that the Lord wants to use for deeper work in our hearts or to give us a lifechanging revelation. Scriptures are central to discovering our identity: through them, we get to know the Father who is our only source.

LEARN TO MAKE DECLARATIONS

Some people may study and meditate on scriptures yet struggle with believing or living them out. This can be due to their present condition, challenges, past experiences, and several other legitimate reasons. Sometimes we need to exercise violence for the Kingdom to manifest in our midst.[161] I can relate to that.

Therefore, I encourage you to practice declaring the word of God over your life and circumstances. There is great power in making declarations, and that is an effective way to wage war using the word. Afterall, scriptures liken the Word of God to a sharp, double-edged sword.[162]

The Lord told Joshua to meditate on the word day and night.[163] The Hebrew word for *"meditate"* here means *"to growl or to speak to oneself."* So, this is not a silent activity. Elsewhere we are told that "faith comes by hearing, and hearing by the word of God."[164]

The first dimension to hearing is by sound. Sometimes reading quietly isn't enough. There are times we need to declare scriptures with force and conviction until the sound of Truth dislodges the lies that sit deep in our subconscious minds.

A day after salvation, I still struggled mightily to believe that I was a child of God and that there was any hope for me. I was reading the word, yet I struggled to believe. And then one morning, I got exceedingly frustrated with the status quo. I resolved to roar the following from the depths of my bowels to the top of my lungs: "Today is the day the Lord has made. I shall rejoice and be glad! I am a son of God; my confidence is in Christ! I can do all things through Christ who gives me strength!" I would repeat this from the moment I woke up throughout the day. I didn't care for the looks of those around me on the streets or in the bus, I was at war!

Pick a verse or passage of your choice that addresses a stronghold in your life and try it. Each time you make a declaration, be intentional to make each utterance more convincing than the last one. If it isn't, stick with it till you sense your spirit man rising from within.

It may feel awkward in the beginning, but over time your thoughts, speech, and actions will grow in alignment. Let us not allow the enemy to rob us of our divine identity. Let us resolve to forcefully take the fight with the sword of the Spirit, the word of God if necessary.

YOUR IDENTITY IS NOT YOUR OCCUPATION

Lastly, it is easy for humans to forge an identity based on their occupation. Our identity in Christ is that of a child of God called to maturity and intimacy with Him. It has nothing to do with our occupation. It has everything to do with the depth and quality of our bond with the Father, through Christ Jesus.

Let us ponder: would we think less of ourselves if we are never given a platform or public recognition for something we've done? If yes, then I pray that the Father saves us from the need to perform and reels us into the bliss of intimacy.

INTIMACY, MORE INTIMACY

Intimacy is developed over time. In the natural, we do not claim to be intimate with people that we have barely met. Often, we consider intimate those with whom we spend a significant amount of time. Not only that, but the time together must result in having insightful and deep knowledge of each other. Likewise, spending time alone with the Lord is the way to grow in intimacy.

For instance, the disciples got more insight into the mind of Jesus than the multitudes. The things that He kept unexplained to others He made known to the ones closest to Him.[165] We were given the Holy Spirit to teach us all things, but it is up to us to draw near and seek His face. The Lord doesn't want us to be estranged from His presence. Instead, He promised that if we come close to Him, He will come close to us.

| GIVE YOURSELF TO PRAYER!

Prayer is vital in the life of any believer. It was the first thing that Jesus' disciples asked the be taught.[166] They probably witnessed the Lord's devotion to prayer, and they surely witnessed the power and authority in which He moved. For one reason or another, they were deeply inspired by His prayer life. No believer can fulfill their destiny without a devoted life of prayer. The greater the calling, the greater the necessity to develop an effective prayer lifestyle.

Billy Graham once said that he never skipped a day without praying. Smith Wigglesworth prayed every twenty minutes, for no more than twenty minutes at a time.[167] It didn't matter if he had guests over at his house, he'd excuse himself every fifteen minutes to pray and then come back to entertain his guest for twenty minutes.

Some may say that they do not need to have a serious prayer life because they are not in ministry or in a position of leadership. Recall that the prophetic leadership process begins with the humility to be led by the Lord ourselves, before we can lead others.[168] If we are truly led by the Lord Jesus, then we will absolutely be drawn to the secret place. Prayer is the way we acknowledge our insufficiency and tap on God's sufficiency.

Ask the Lord what He desires for your prayer life. Then ask for the grace to honor it. It will transform your life. Be prepared for opposition, for the enemy and the flesh will oppose your desire and resolve.[169] He knows the power of prayer is effective to repel the kingdom of darkness and advance the kingdom of God.

| PRACTICE LISTENING

Prayer is our means of communication with the Father, and it is a two-way street. Allow time for input from the Lord as much as you output. Some of the most effective communicators aren't those who talk all the time, but those who have trained themselves to be great listeners.

We often do not receive an answer to our prayers due to our microwave mindsets. We talk (for most of us in the form of babbling and complaining), and once we are done making noise, we get up and leave. How rude! How would we like it if someone did that to us?

We often do not give God time to speak back to us. Could it be that we are more interested in being heard than we are in listening? When you are done praying and making your requests known, practice remaining quiet before the Lord for at least as much time as you spoke. I promise you; your prayer life will enter a new dimension. I personally pray first, and then meditate on scriptures to hear the word of the Lord. Without fail, He always gives me fresh manna.

LOVE PRAYER AND STAND

Let prayer not be something that we do out of obligation or as a ritual. Let us be motivated by our love and longing to fellowship with the One who loved us first. Furthermore, we need to realize that prayerlessness does not exist in scriptures. According to Jesus, we are either prayerful or we are fainting.

Prayer will give you the stature to stand before the principalities that are ruling over your given sphere of influence. You will not fulfill prophetic destiny without a strong prayer life, you can book it. There are countless resources on effective prayer, starting with the model that Jesus gave us. The execution of these things will vary from one person to another, but the point is, we need to pray regularly![170]

KNOWING THE CALL ON YOUR LIFE

This is perhaps the most popular topic of interest in our generation. This is true in Christianity as well as in the world. It is in part because human beings have a desire for significance. Everyone on planet earth desires to achieve something. As believers, before we aspire to lead and while we are in leadership, it is important to know what we are primary called to.

We are called to be conformed to the image of Christ, which is the highest calling. Then we are called to love God with all our heart and with all our soul and with all our strength and with all our mind. Following that, we are also called to love our neighbor as ourselves.[171]

Furthermore, we saw earlier that Jesus proves our love by our obedience. We are children of God, and we are called to keep the Lord's commands. Anything else flows out of that place. Many

Christians wrongly believe that obedience to God begins with doing. Once again, this is performance driven.

Furthermore, this kind of thinking violates the divine protocol. Before the power to do anything was given to us, the first power God gave to those who believe in Jesus is the power to become His sons. We fulfill prophetic destiny as we move in the power of sonship. You will be in grave danger if you venture into activities without having a sure footing on the Rock of salvation.

| CALLING AND COMMUNITY

One of the keys to knowing our calling is to be part of a community of believers. That is important because we are designed to be completed by others, and to complete others. We may sometimes have a sense of destiny and it takes a fellow brother (or sister) to confirm what we may have sensed all along.

Community is a wonderful place to receive inspired words, encouragement, correction, confirmation, and even direction at times. The Lord revealed the prophetic destiny over my life and confirmed my wife's identity through an angelic encounter. This encounter took place during an intimate retreat with other believers.

Also, do not despise inspired messages from others but be quick to evaluate them – holding on to what is good, but keeping away from every form of evil.[172] Prophetic words are usually meant to confirm what we knew all along. Sometimes a prophetic word may come to you that does not fit anything that the Lord has already spoken to you privately. You may not reject it, but you must pray it through, evaluate it using the word of God, and bring it to a mentor or a seasoned prophetic voice in your life for further insight.

| GO FOR THE FATHER'S VOICE

If we rely on another person's revelation, we may not have the backbone necessary to persevere. Jesus called John the Baptist the greatest prophet born of a woman. Before he baptized Jesus, he prophesied concerning Jesus' identity and destiny aloud and publicly in front of many.

None of what he said was a surprise to Jesus, just a confirmation of what He already knew. Yet despite all of that, the Father Himself found it necessary to affirm Jesus directly. You must learn to seek the face of God to hear what the Father says concerning His will for you.

In my case, I have received several prophetic words of destiny by high profile, seasoned, and trustworthy prophets. If I were to mention their names you would know who they are. These words have been for the most part fully accurate and confirmed one or more aspects of the word that was spoken to me in my angelic encounter. Yet, I was still not firmly established on my path. At times I would doubt that I was called when hardships came.

So, one day I was determined to not leave my room until God spoke to me directly concerning His will for me. I honored the prophets and the angel, but I needed my spiritual confidence to be built upon the Rock Himself. After about seven hours of straight and intense prayer, the Word of the Lord finally came into my room and spoke three times! The word that the Lord Himself gave me during that encounter has been the Rock I stand upon whenever the enemy tries to plant seeds of doubts in my mind.

By now, if you were diligent to study, pray and meditate through the concepts and principles that were presented in this book, Holy Spirit would whisper to your heart concerning the will of God for you. If in doubt, lock yourself up in prayer and seek His face until He speaks.

Yes, the times demand that we mature and no longer rely on others to reveal the mind of God to us. What will you do when you are called upon to lead others to their place of divine fulfillment if you do not know how to seek the face of God for yourself?

If that statement provoked you to put this book down momentarily and to storm the gates of heaven in prayer, then do so. Finally, learn from mentors, and look to mentor others. You will discover certain aspects of your calling as you invest yourself in the lives of others.

Marching Orders

| SUBMIT TO THE PROPHETIC VISION

Trapped inside of you may be one of the most incredible gifts the world desperately needs. Let us not add to the enormous amounts of wealth that are currently buried in the graveyard due to fear, ignorance, or indifference. Instead, let us deny the graveyards of our wealth.

Our goal in life should not be to live a long life or to obtain a longevity trophy in ministry. Our aim should be to depart from the earth empty, knowing that we have given it everything that the Creator intended us to give. If we can redirect our focus in such a way, then we will be less terrified of death.

Jesus lived for thirty-three years, and His earthly ministry only lasted three years. Yet He died empty by accomplishing everything that was spoken of Him from the beginning. He had a short-lived earthly existence and by far the most impactful three years of ministry in recorded history.

We are still reaping the fruit of the Lord's ministry because of His penetrating vision and His diligence to the Father's business. It is said that "Without a prophetic vision, the people throw off all restraint."[173] A life without restraint is a sure path to destruction. Death doesn't always occur at the end of life. Many of us are walking through life aimlessly, tossed here and there by any kind of new wind.

The Lord came that we may have life, and life more abundantly. Along the way, we are also destined to communicate His life in a way that significantly influences our generation. Unfortunately, we cannot impart what we do not possess. It is time that we behold our Lord as the ultimate leader that He is, and that we resolve to actively submit our lives to His redemptive vision for the earth.

| IMPARTATION WORKS BEST WITH REVELATION

It is time that we begin to choose revelation out of intimacy over impartation. I sense that one of the main reasons the church has been ineffective in producing prophetic leaders is the proliferation of spiritual impartations. Do not get me wrong, I love impartation. In fact, I know you will receive a serious impartation if you seriously take the content of this book to heart.

However, we have created a culture in which folks desire impartation at the expense of personal revelation. This is significant because there can be no boldness without revelation. The church lacks backbone and boldness in part because we are obtaining gifts from others without going through a process.

I have seen people ask me to impart my spiritual authority to them, saying "Impart to us. We want everything that you have." Not a problem, but once I mentioned that imparting everything that I have might come with seasons of rejection, brokenness, travail, spiritual warfare, and trials attached to it, they would say "No, we only want the fun stuff." My response to that type of request is and will always be a resounding "No."

I will always impart spiritual gifts to those who are genuine, as the Lord leads me. But I will not participate in adding to the large number of Simon the sorcerers who run around with giftings without a genuine love for the Lord and for His people.

| YOU'RE THE LORD'S MAGISTRATE

We are on the cusp of the greatest harvest in human history. With such multitude, the Lord is looking for valiant people who are willing to die to selfish ambition, stand in the gap, and engage with prophetic vision. Furthermore, He is looking to raise leaders that are burning with His desire for justice and righteousness in the nations of the earth.

Confrontation is inevitable, even within the church. There is now a clear line of demarcation being drawn between sheep and goats. Soon enough, we will no longer be able to remain lukewarm regarding the spiritual and cultural war that will usher in the harvest.

The Lord is looking for people that are immersed in the consuming reality of His love. Furthermore, He is longing for us to realize that His word is truly the final authority on any matter. Your life is a prophecy waiting for fulfillment and the author of that script is none other than the King of all kings.

| THE KING'S DECREE WILL STAND

History among other things taught us that a king's word had supreme authority over any matter under his jurisdiction, or within his kingdom. It was even common for kings to be followed by scribes who would literally write down every word spoken by the king.

This is because a word coming out of his mouth was as good as a decree and no one could bypass it. This, however, wasn't an invention of men, but a principle established by God Himself: "For the word of a king is authoritative and powerful, and who will say to him, "What are you doing?"[174]

Now, it is well documented throughout scriptures that God is a King. In fact, Psalms 47:7 declares that "God is the King of all the earth" and that Jesus is the Ruler of the kings of the earth as the *"KING OF KINGS"*.[175] Additionally, the word of God declares that every governing authority on the earth is appointed by God Himself.[176]

This means that God's word has the power and authority to override the words and actions of any other man or leader, plain and simple. This is especially true when the words uttered by men and leaders exalt themselves against the knowledge of Christ. This includes our very own words and beliefs towards ourselves, others, and circumstances.

Once we made the decision to believe and follow Jesus Christ as Lord and Savior, we became citizens of the Kingdom of God. Just as every nation on earth has laws, the Kingdom of God has principles in place that govern our walk here on earth. God is THE KING above all: "The earth is the Lord's, and the fullness thereof, the world and those who live there."[177] And for that reason, His word is the final say in any matter concerning the believer's life.

I, therefore, invite you to dust off those prophetic words and promises that you have shelved in the names of fear and unbelief. In case you haven't joined the Kingdom yet, I invite you to dust the world off your shoulders and embark on the greatest adventure you will ever take part in.

| RULE LIKE YOUR FATHER!

Concerning fear, allow me to remind you of your identity. As children of God, we became royalty at the new birth, thanks to Jesus' death and resurrection. As a risen Savior, He became the First Born of a new breed of people. Paul in his letter to the Romans indeed states that God the Father determined whom He knew in advance to be conformed to the pattern (image) of His Son; so that He might be the firstborn among many brothers.

That last sentence is one that many have difficulty grasping even among believers, so I'll attempt to say it in plain language: Jesus is our big Brother, as well as He is our Lord, Savior, and Groomsman!

In a much broader sense, those who are in Christ are one with Him! I have observed that in our earthly customs one can only be called firstborn if they have siblings born after them from the same father. Similarly, in a spiritual sense we are God's own seed and born of Him for we received His Spirit, Who makes us sons and by Whose power we cry out "Abba!" that is, "Dear Father!" [178]

Based on this premise and staying true to our context: since He is King, then we too are destined for royal status, and since He is God

– this might offend the religious spirit - then we too are gods on the earth. That was not a typo or blasphemy, it is what our Father's word says! The psalmist says in chapter 82, verse 26: "My decree is: "You are gods, and all of you are sons of the Most High."

YE ARE GODS

I find it interesting that Jesus in His infinite wisdom chose to quote this verse in response to the Judeans who were out to stone Him, accusing Him to make Himself out to be God, which He never did though He was God in the flesh: He constantly deferred all the glory to His Father and never attempted to ignore the Holy Spirit. We are mandated to do the same: after all, we are to conform our ways to Jesus' pattern.

Make no mistake: Jesus is the only Man who can ever be God and worshiped as such. No other man dead or alive can ever claim that title, yet He calls us gods. If we are born of Him, then we must partake in His nature and attributes. A lion begets a cub, and the cub eventually grows into a lion. You get the picture.

The translated word for gods here is the Hebrew word *"Elohim"* which means *gods, judges, rulers, mighty ones,* and is occasionally applied by way of deference to magistrates. This word "Elohim" is first used of God in Genesis 1:1 "In the beginning God (Elohim) created the heavens and the earth."

Let us follow this trail and investigate John 1:1 "In the beginning was the Word." By comparison, the Word is the one who created the heavens, the earth, and all of creation. Now, this "*Word*" is the Greek word "*logos,*" which the Greeks understood as the *spoken and unspoken* word. God gave existence to the entire creation by releasing the Word and that Word was alive and active before He became flesh.

God's word has the ability not only to give life but to also become alive. We better be convinced that the word of prophetic destiny that He has spoken over our lives also has similar creative potential. We only need to learn how to war with the prophetic words[179] given to us because they carry the authority of the Ruler of the universe.

HIS LOVE WILL KEEP YOU

Lastly, love is the ultimate driving force for prophetic leadership. By love, I clearly mean *agape* love, the perfect love of the God, which is benevolent in nature. It is the Lord's inherent character and the predominant tendency of His Spirit. "There is no fear in love. But perfect love drives out fear."[180]

According to God, fear only exists outside of Him because He is the personification of love. Fear robs us of the fulfillment of the Lord's purposes for our lives. It is crucial that we discover by way of experience that His love is an unmatched force that guards His word against any opposition.

Jesus came to fulfill what was written about Him. Nothing and no one could take His life until He completed everything He was purposed to accomplish. The Father simply wouldn't allow it because the Son had determined to fulfill scriptures which testified of Him. And because Jesus had experiential knowledge of the love of the Father, He had complete assurance regardless of the situation He was in. The Lord has also written our days and lives' journey in a book.[181] And He gradually reveals us pages and chapters as we intimately walk with Him.

If our lives are hidden in Christ, then we also have a purpose to fulfill on the earth. More importantly, we also have the assurance that if we are genuinely about the Father's business, no man or circumstance can rob us of our lives without His permission.

Numerous times the enemy attempted to kill the Lord Jesus but every time the Father ensured that no one could. One of the most dramatic attempts took place in John 18:4-6: "Jesus, knowing all that was about to befall Him, went out to them and said, whom are you seeking? They answered Him, Jesus the Nazarene. Jesus said to them, I am He. When Jesus said to them, I am He, they lurched backward and fell to the ground." The word was that He was going to offer Himself. The Father wasn't going to allow any man to glory in capturing Jesus: His script had to be fulfilled to the letter. So can yours.

WHERE DO YOU STAND?

The Lord Jesus is still on the throne and His word is infallible. Therefore, let us wake up out of our deep slumber and lay hold of our prophetic destiny with boldness and courage. Prophetic leaders' humility is rooted in their confidence in the Lord's ability to perform His own word.

Fear and pride creep in when we begin to look at our own ability. The Lord has set our lives in motion with a Word that no one can stop. He has also hedged our lives with a fiery love that nothing can extinguish.

Will you give in to fear and passively allow the ungodly to rule your generation? Or will you resolve to proactively engage the marvelous vision that the Lord longs to fulfill on the earth with you? Those who want to protect their lives will lose it. Those who willingly surrender their lives will ultimately find them.

There are people in governments, businesses, families, schools, nations, and even churches that are waiting for you to emerge as a catalyst to their redemption. Will you answer the royal call and let God use your life to move His people to their divine inheritance? Or will the champion in you cower to fear and return to a life of insignificance rooted in selfish and worthless ambition? That is really what it comes down to. The choice is yours.

CONCLUSION

Prophetic leadership is a process that originates with God. It is the way God prepares the prophetic people He wants to use in a generation. He trains men to walk before Him before He can release them to walk before men. His goal is to first cause the man or woman that He desires to use to hear His voice. Then, He shapes His voice within the life of the individual.

In other words, the life of the prophetic leader brings forth the word of the Lord. Throughout this process, the Lord intends to lead us to our place of divine inheritance, which is simply a life consistent with His will for us.

The prophetic leadership process is completed once the individual embraces the dealings of the Lord in their life and engages the prophetic vision that the Lord has for their life. At this point, the individual no longer lives for themselves. God begins to further His agenda on the earth through them, which consists of leading others to their own place of divine fulfillment. However, such place of fulfilment can only be found in Christ.

This means that ultimately prophetic leaders are not only concerned about the fulfilment of their individual assignment on the earth. They understand that the heavens rejoice the more when their lives become a gift to humanity.

Prophetic leadership is therefore a process and a way of life for the prophet and a prophetic person in general. The intensity of the dealings in one's life are stronger depending on the weight of the calling. In fact, although all prophetic people endure dealings, those who are called to be prophets will experience those dealings more intensely.

It is important to understand that your dealings are not a punishment, but a sign of approval because God has selected you for a splendid work. Therefore, He desires for you to fulfill prophetic destiny even more than you do, and He uses these dealings to form the character necessary to sustain the weight of glory that you are meant to carry.

We must acknowledge that the Lord is not just interested in using us. More importantly He wants us to make ourselves known to Him. The dealings are often an excuse the Father will use to draw us to Him. In all things, draw to the Lord and desire to be intimate with Him. If you can stick with Him and fall in love with Him during those trying times, then you will taste and see that He is good.

We are on the cusp of the greatest harvest in human history. We are also nearing the return of the Lord, and things will increasingly be darker in the world. But you must remember that your Light has already come and now is your time to shine. The Lord is raising up a new standard on the earth, and you happen to be alive for this purpose.

You are not allowed to disqualify yourself, because He chose you first. You may not give into doubt because His word is set to accomplish what He has spoken concerning the body of Christ and concerning you. I pray you can use this book as training material, and that the stories therein can be a source of inspiration and impartation. Now, dig in your own wells so that others may be refreshed by your overflow.

AFTERWORD

Prophet Kenneth Hagin said, "To obey the Voice of God, you must know the voice of God. He contacts you through your spirit – not through your mind, and not through your body – because He is a Spirit."

Ulrich has written a sharp, clear exposition of these same words with a passion for God's people to equip and stir them to have a "hearing ear" to hear and then obey the voice of the Master. Part of the prophetic gifting is positioning our ear to God and in turn use our prophetic voice to speak God's words into the hearts of men. Ulrich's heart of love and compassion towards God's holy people are shown through his writings, and he does so by helping you to sharpen your ability to hear God's voice and learning to flow in the gifts such as words of knowledge, words of wisdom and prophecy.

Yes, there may be problems and abuses within the contemporary prophetic movement. Sadly, in certain arenas the prophetic movement has been used to try to make us feel good about ourselves or to build self-esteem, and it has been used mistakenly in an attempt to reveal the depth, or lack thereof, of our spirituality. But the mature believer understands two key principles – this gifting is God-given for the purpose of winning the lost by using the prophetic. The prophetic ministry is powerful and very precious to the Lord, so as believers we must realize that spiritual gifts are not toys, they are tools, to equip the body of Christ for an abundant Kingdom harvest!

The second key principles known to the matured Christian believer is that using our prophetic giftings is not difficult or complicated – it is actually quite simple. It is learning to accurately hear the voice of our Shepherd, hearing His thoughts and intentions toward His creation, and then using the prophetic to encourage, build-up and equip His people.

As you read the pages of this anointed book, may the words burn inside you to encounter fresh passion for Jesus, passion to better and more accurately hear His voice. Like Ulrich, I too believe that God is preparing you to do amazing Kingdom works and that can only be accomplished with the same kind of passion that Brother Ulrich carries. May you grow into the fullness of your spiritual sonship and into a place of Christian maturity where you no longer struggle to hear His voice and where you're always-answer to him will become, "Speak Lord, for your servant is listening."

Prophetic Revivalists Tom & Susie Scarrella
St. Paul, MN
www.sharethefire.org

Our vision and mission statement: www.royalheirs.org/statements

Contact us via: www.royalheirs.org/contact or contact@royalheirs.org

Follow Ulrich Tofack: @UlrichTofack on Facebook and Instagram

Subscribe our YouTube channel: Dr Ulrich Tofack / Royal Heirs

To donate or partner with Ulrich Tofack: www.royalheirs.org/give

BIBLIOGRAPHY

1. Dye, Colin. Smith Wigglesworth on Prayer. Colin Dye (2013). https://www.colindye.com/2013/03/04/smith-wigglesworth-on-prayer.
2. Joyner, Rick. Leadership: The Power of a Creative Life. 3rd ed. Fort Mill: MorningStar Publications, Inc., 2001
3. Joyner, Rick. The Fire That Could Not Die. Fort Mill: MorningStar Publications, 1998
4. Joyner, Rick. Interview with Michael Fickess & Ulrich Tofack, master's in leadership Part 1. Oak Video #227, The Oak Initiative (2019). http://www.theoakinitiative.org/oak-video-227#.XWsCaShKiUk.
5. Liardon, Roberts. Smith Wigglesworth: On Prayer, Power, and Miracles. Shippensburg: Destiny Image Publishers, 2006.
6. Lucas, Jim. Equal & Opposite Reactions: Newton's Third Law of Motion. Live Science (2017). https://www.livescience.com/46561-newton-third-law.html. Newton's Third Law of Motion.
7. Mansfield, Stephen. Never Give In: The Extraordinary Character of Winston Churchill. Nashville: Cumberland House, 1995.
8. Munroe, Myles. Becoming a Leader. New Kensington: Whitaker House, 2009.
9. Roosevelt, Theodore. (1910). Citizenship in a Republic.

10. Sandys, J. & Henley, W. God & Churchill: How the Great Leader's Sense of Divine Destiny Changed His Troubled World and Offers Hope for Ours. Carol Stream: Tyndale Momentum, 2015.
11. Sohn, Paul. Top 15 Myles Munroe Quotes of All-Time. Paul Sohn (2014). https://paulsohn.org/top-15-myles-munroe-quotes-of-all-time.
12. Tofack, Ulrich. Cultivating Your Inner Man. Royal Insights (2018). https://www.royalheirs.org/single-post/2018/05/28/Cultivating-your-inner-man.
13. Price, Paula A. The Prophet's Dictionary: The Ultimate Guide to Supernatural Wisdom. rev. and expanded ed. Whitaker House, 2006.
14. Sandford, R. Loren. *Understanding Prophetic People*: blessings and problems with the prophetic gift. Chosen Books, 2007.
15. Stern, David H. *The Complete Jewish Study Bible: Insights for Jews and Christians, Illuminating the Jewishness of God's Word*, Hendrickson Publishers Marketing, LLC, 2016.
16. Merriam-Webster.com. 2021 [online]. To lead, https://www.dictionary.com/browse/lead
17. Malcolm, Lynne. "Research Says Young People Today Are More Narcissistic than Ever." *ABC Radio National*, 16 May 2014, www.abc.net.au/radionational/programs/allinthemind/young-people-today-are-more-narcissistic-than-ever/5457236.
18. "H5095 - Nāhal - Strong's Hebrew Lexicon (KJV)." *Blue Letter Bible*, www.blueletterbible.org//lang/lexicon/lexicon.cfm?Strongs=H5095&t=KJV. Accessed 29 May 2022.
19. Munroe, Myles. *The Spirit of Leadership*. New Kensington, Pa., Whitaker House, 2005.
20. Heschel, Abraham Joshua. *The Prophets*. 1962. 1st ed., New York, Perennial Classics, 2001

21. Hackett, Conrad, and David McClendon. "World's Largest Religion by Population Is Still Christianity." Pew Research Center, 31 May 2020, www.pewresearch.org/fact-tank/2017/04/05/christians-remain-worlds-largest-religious-group-but-they-are-declining-in-europe.
22. Bidmead, Julye. "Women and Wells in the Hebrew Bible." www.bibleodyssey.org, www.bibleodyssey.org:443/en/places/related-articles/women-and-wells-in-the-hebrew-bible. Accessed 29 May 2022.
23. "H3290 - Yaʿăqōḇ - Strong's Hebrew Lexicon (KJV)." *Blue Letter Bible*, www.blueletterbible.org//lang/lexicon/lexicon.cfm?Strongs=H3290&t=KJV. Accessed 29 May 2022.
24. "Life Expectancy at Birth." *Worldbank.org*, 2022, data.worldbank.org/indicator/SP.DYN.LE00.IN. Accessed 29 May 2022.
25. Conner, Bobby. *Dread Champions: Lionlike Warriors - Preparing a Valiant Victorious Generation of Overcomers*. Bullard, Texas, Eagles View Ministries, 2020.
26. Johnson, Jeremiah. *Cleansing and Igniting the Prophetic*. Destiny Image, 2018.
27. Johnson, Jeremiah. *Walking in the Prophetic Anointing*, Compact Disc Audio Teaching.
28. "H5650 - ʿeḇeḏ - Strong's Hebrew Lexicon (KJV)." *Blue Letter Bible*, www.blueletterbible.org/lexicon/h5650/kjv/wlc/0-1/. Accessed 29 May 2022.
29. "Religion | Definition of Religion by Lexico." *Lexico Dictionaries | English*, 2019, www.lexico.com/en/definition/religion.
30. "Definition of CULTIVATE." www.merriam-Webster.com, www.merriam-webster.com/dictionary/cultivate.
31. Goll, James W. *Lifestyle of a Prophet - a 21-Day Journey to Embracing Your Calling*. Baker Publishing Group, 2013

ENDNOTES

Part I

1. See Romans 5:3-4.
2. Proverbs 21:1.
3. Romans 13:1.
4. See Jeremiah 51:24-29.
5. Romans 13:12, CJB.
6. See Philippians 1:6; Zechariah 4:6.
7. David H. Stern, The Complete Jewish Study Bible: Insights for Jews and Christians, Illuminating the Jewishness of God's Word, (Hendrickson Publishers Marketing, LLC, 2016), 27.
8. See Genesis 20:1-20.
9. "To lead." Merriam-Webster.com. 2021. https://www.dictionary.com/browse/lead (23 March 2021).
10. See 2 Timothy 3:2.
11. Lynne Malcolm, *"Research Says Young People Today are More Narcissistic Than Ever"*, All in the Mind, 19 August 2014, https://www.abc.nct.au/radionational/programs/allinthemind/young-people-today-are-more-narcissistic-than-ever/5457236. Accessed 15 Oct 2021.

12 "H5095 - nāhal - Strong's Hebrew Lexicon (KJV)." Blue Letter Bible. Accessed 23 Mar 2021. https://www.blueletterbible.org//lang/lexicon/lexicon.cfm?Strongs=H5095&t=KJV
13 See Genesis 32:24-32, Genesis 33:4-12.
14 Psalms 23:2.
15 Jim Lucas, *Equal & Opposite Reactions: Newton's Third Law of Motion.*, Live Science, September 25, 2017, Accessed May 05, 2019, https://www.livescience.com/46561-newton-third-law.html.
16 Romans 1:20.
17 See Genesis 1:3-4.
18 See Isaiah 6:3.
19 John 1:5, CJB.
20 See John 8:12.
21 Proverbs 8:22, KJV.
22 Genesis 1:4, CJB.
23 Isaiah 60:2-3, NIV.
24 Dr. Myles Munroe, *The Spirit of Leadership: Cultivating the Attitudes that Influence Human Action,* (Whitaker House, 2005), 103.
25 See Revelation 21:23, 22:5.
26 See Ephesians 5:8-13.
27 Rick Joyner, *Leadership: The Power of a Creative Life*, 3rd ed. (MorningStar Publications, Inc., 2001), 12.
28 Jonathan Sandys & Wallace Henley, *God & Churchill: How the Great Leader's Sense of Divine Destiny Changed His Troubled World and Offers Hope for Ours*, (Tyndale Momentum, 2015), 4, 8.

29 Abraham Joshua Heschel, *The Prophets*, 1st ed. (Perennial Classics, 2001), 14, 19.
30 Stephen Mansfield, Never Give In: *The Extraordinary Character of Winston Churchill* (Nashville: Cumberland House, 1995), 39.
31 Sandys and Henley, *God & Churchill*, 8.
32 See John 10:10.
33 2 Corinthians 11:14, CJB.
34 See Isaiah 14:13-14, Ezekiel 28:13-14.
35 See 2 Corinthians 2:11.
36 Sandys and Henley, *God & Churchill*, 62, 63.
37 See Matthew 21:12-13; Mark 11:15-18.
38 See Revelation 19:11-15; 1 Corinthians 15:25.
39 Proverbs 8:13, NIV.
40 Myles Munroe, *Becoming a Leader* (New Kensington: Whitaker House, 2009), 59.
41 See Numbers 22:21-39.
42 See Luke 19:40.
43 See Revelation 21:8.
44 See Matthew 28:19-20.
45 See 1 Corinthians 12:28, 1 Corinthians 14:1, 31.
46 Matthew 4:4, NKJV.
47 See Proverbs 29:2.
48 Paul Sohn, *Top 15 Myles Munroe Quotes of All-Time*, https://paulsohn.org/top-15-myles-munroe-quotes-of-all-time/, (Accessed 29 Sep. 2018).
49 Myles Munroe, *Becoming a Leader*, 59.

Part II

50   John 3:3

51   Conrad Hackett and David McClendon, *"World's Largest Religion by Population Is Still Christianity,"* Pew Research Center (Pew Research Center, May 31, 2020), https://www.pewresearch.org/fact-tank/2017/04/05/christians-remain-worlds-largest-religious-group-but-they-are-declining-in-europe/, (Accessed 14 Apr. 2021)

52   See Genesis 12:1.

53   See Genesis 13.

54   See Genesis 13:5-9.

55   Sandys and Henley, *God & Churchill*, 5.

56   R. Loren Sandford, *Understanding Prophetic People*, 37

57   R. Loren Sandford, *Understanding Prophetic People*, 38.

58   R. Loren Sandford, *Understanding Prophetic People*, 33.

59   Myles Munroe, *The spirit of Leadership*, 170, 171, 184.

60   Genesis 24:11, NET.

61   Julye Bidmead, *"Women and Wells in the Hebrew Bible"*, n.p. [cited 6 May 2021]. Online: https://www.bibleodyssey.org:443/en/places/related-articles/women-and-wells-in-the-hebrew-bible

62   See John 4:1-42.

63   "H3290 - Ya⊠ăqō⊠ - Strong's Hebrew Lexicon (KJV)." Blue Letter Bible. Accessed 7 May 2021. https://www.blueletterbible.org//lang/lexicon/lexicon.cfm?Strongs=H3290&t=KJV

64   R. Loren Sandford, *Understanding Prophetic People*, 167.

65   James 4:6.

66   See 1 Corinthians 15:33.

ENDNOTES

67 See Luke 15:11-31.
68 See Proverbs 18:16.
69 Matthew 25:34-46.
70 John 14:6.
71 See Luke 22:24-27.
72 Myles Munroe, *The Spirit of Leadership*, 187.
73 The World Bank | Data, *Life Expectancy at Birth*, https://data.worldbank.org/indicator/SP.DYN.LE00.IN.
74 2 Corinthians 1:4.
75 Psalm 38:22, AMP.
76 See Matthew 6:7.
77 See Isaiah 43:18-19.
78 See Psalm 30:5.
79 Paula A. Price PhD, *The Prophet's Dictionary: The Ultimate Guide to Supernatural Wisdom*, (Whitaker House, 2006), 429.
80 R. Loren Sanford, Understanding Prophetic People, 167.
81 Isaiah 61:3.
82 Bobby Conner, *Dread Champions: Lionlike Warriors - Preparing a Valiant Victorious Generation of Overcomers*, (Eagles View Ministries, 2020), 39.
83 See 1 John 1:8.
84 See 1 Peter 1:15, AMP.
85 See Romans 8:26.
86 Bobby Conner, *Dread Champions*, 40.
87 James 4:8.
88 John 4:24.
89 Jeremiah Johnson, *Cleansing and Igniting the Prophetic: An Urgent Wake-Up Call*, (Destiny Image, 2018), 61.
90 2 Corinthians 5:17, NIV.
91 James 1:14.

92   Mark 10:15.
93   See Ephesians 3:20.
94   Hebrews 11:10, CJB.
95   Mark 9:23, CJB.
96   See John 17:3.
97   Isaiah 45:2-3, NIV.
98   See Genesis 22:1-2.
99   See Matthew 4:1.
100   See Genesis 37.
101   Hebrews 13:8.
102   See Jeremiah 17:5, 9.
103   See Proverbs 18:22.
104   See Deuteronomy 26:18.
105   Matthew 16:21-23
106   Jeremiah Johnson, *Walking in the Prophetic Anointing*, Compact Disc Audio Teaching.
107   See Matthew 4:5-7.
108   See John 17:3.
109   Galatians 5:22-23
110   See Genesis 22:2.
111   See Exodus 18:4.
112   See Genesis 24:1-20.
113   Revelation 19:7, CJB.
114   See 2 Corinthians 3:18.
115   See Revelation 19:6-9.
116   See 1 Corinthians 6:17.
117   See 1 Corinthians 2:9.
118   Psalm 115:16, AMP.

Part III

119   See Matthew 6:10-11.
120   Amos 3:7, NIV.
121   "H5650 - ☐e☐e☐ - Strong's Hebrew Lexicon (KJV)." Blue Letter Bible. Accessed 17 May 2022. https://www.blueletterbible.org/lexicon/h5650/kjv/wlc/0-1/.
122   2 Corinthians 2:16.
123   See 1 Corinthians 12:10.
124   See Psalm 89:14.
125   See Psalms 97:10.
126   Lexico, *Definition of religion in English*, Powered by Oxford, https://www.lexico.com/en/definition/religion
127   Abraham Heschel, *The Prophets*, 1st ed. (Perennial Classics, 2001), 4.
128   Myles Munroe, *Becoming a Leader*, 69.
129   Zechariah 4:6.
130   See Isaiah 42:8.
131   Genesis 17:17.
132   See 1 Corinthians 1:27.
133   Judges 6:15-16, NIV.
134   Romans 8:28, CJB.
135   Theodore Roosevelt, *Citizenship in a Republic*, 1910 Speech.
136   Isaiah 46:10, ESV.
137   Rick Joyner, *The Fire That Could Not Die* (MorningStar Publications, 1998), 15.
138   Proverbs 12:11, CJB.
139   See Proverbs 28:19.
140   See Genesis 2:15.

141 "Definition of CULTIVATE", https://www.merriam-webster.com/dictionary/cultivate
142 Ulrich Tofack, *Cultivating your inner man* (Royal Heirs Ministries, 2018), https://www.royalheirs.org/single-post/2018/05/28/Cultivating-your-inner-man.
143 Rick Joyner, *Leadership: The Power of a Creative Life*, 14.
144 See Luke 12:7.
145 Paula A. Price, *The Prophet's Dictionary*, 593.
146 Ephesians 2:10, NIV.
147 See Matthew 15:14-30.
148 James W. Goll, *The Lifestyle of a Prophet: A 21-Day Journey to Embracing Your Calling*, (Chosen Book, 2001, 2013), 215.
149 See John 15:8.
150 Proverbs 25:2, NIV.
151 Proverbs 29:25, CJB
152 1 Corinthians 6:12, CJB.
153 Rick Joyner, *The Fire That Could Not Die*, 11.
154 James W. Goll, *The Lifestyle of a Prophet*, 216.
155 See Romans 16:25.
156 Roberts Liardon, *Smith Wigglesworth: On Prayer, Power, and Miracles* (Destiny Image, 2006), 47.
157 See Daniel 10.
158 See 1 Samuel 17.
159 See James 2:19.
160 2 Timothy 3:16, CJB.
161 See Matthew 11:12.
162 Hebrews 4:12.
163 See Joshua 1:8.
164 See Romans 10:17, NIV.
165 See Mark 4:34.

166 See Luke 11:1.
167 Colin Dye, *Smith Wigglesworth On Prayer* (2013), https://www.colindye.com/2013/03/04/smith-wigglesworth-on-prayer/.
168 See James 4:10.
169 See Matthew 26:40.
170 1 Thessalonians 5:17.
171 Luke 10:27.
172 1 Thessalonians 5:19-22.

Part IV

173 Proverbs 29:18, CJB.
174 Ecclesiastes 8:4, AMP.
175 Revelation 19:16, CJB.
176 See Romans 13:1.
177 Psalm 24:1.
178 Romans 8:15, CJB.
179 See 1 Timothy 1:18.
180 1 John 4:18, NIV.
181 See Psalm 139:16-17

Made in the USA
Columbia, SC
18 November 2023

26702772R00120